Good Housekeeping FAVORITE RECIPES

ROAST IT!

Roast Capon with
Baby Carrots

Good Housekeeping FAVORITE RECIPES

ROAST IT!

More Than 140 Savory Recipes for Meat, Poultry, Seafood & Vegetables

HEARST BOOKS

A DIVISION OF STERLING PUBLISHING CO., INC.

NEW YORK

Ellen Levine	**Editor in Chief**
Susan Westmoreland	**Food Director**
Susan Deborah Goldsmith	**Associate Food Director**
Delia Hammock	**Nutrition Director**
Sharon Franke	**Food Appliances Director**
Richard Eisenberg	**Special Projects Director**
Marilu Lopez	**Design Director**

Photography Credits on page 222
Book design by Renato Stanisic

Library of Congress
Cataloging-in-Publication Data

Roast it! : Good housekeeping favorite recipes /
the editors of Good housekeeping.
p. cm.
Includes index.
ISBN 1-58816-479-9
1. Roasting (Cookery) I. Good housekeeping.
TX690.R63 2005
641.7′1—dc22

2004024743

10 9 8 7 6 5 4 3 2 1

Published by Hearst Books
A Division of Sterling Publishing Co., Inc.
387 Park Avenue South, New York, NY 10016

For information about custom editions,
special sales, premium and corporate purchases,
please contact Sterling Special Sales Department
at 800-805-5489 or
specialsales@sterlingpub.com.

Distributed in Canada by Sterling Publishing
c/o Canadian Manda Group, 165 Dufferin Street
Toronto, Ontario, Canada M6K 3H6

Distributed in Australia by Capricorn Link
(Australia) Pty. Ltd.
P.O. Box 704, Windsor, NSW 2756 Australia

Manufactured in China

ISBN 1-58816-479-9

CONTENTS

Turkey Breast with
Mushroom Filling

FOREWORD

At *Good Housekeeping,* we find roasting to be a delicious solution to everyday cooking. It's a way to get dinner on the table with no-fuss and with superb results! Meat and poultry come out of the oven crisply browned on the outside, tender and juicy on the inside. Oven-roasted fish stays moist and succulent—we'll tell you exactly how to time it—while vegetables roasted at high heat are especially sweet and tender.

No wonder many of America's favorite meals—Thanksgiving turkey, holiday roast beef, Easter ham, golden roast chicken, or spring leg of lamb—are roasted in the oven. And many of these are made from recipes that have been handed down for generations.

We all look forward to these special holiday hams and turkeys, but don't reserve roasting for just weekends and celebrations. Once it's in the oven, a roasted dinner cooks virtually on its own; all you have to do is check the time.

On the pages that follow, you'll find a wonderful variety of recipes to choose from. Some are simple—perfect for a weeknight meal—others are show-stopping holiday feasts. Best of all, each and every recipe has been triple-tested to ensure that you get perfect results every time.

Susan Westmoreland
Food Director, Good Housekeeping

Roast Chicken with Squash

READY TO ROAST

Successful roasts have come from ovens of all kinds, but it is important to know something about how your oven works before starting. In Colonial America, meats were first roasted on a spit over the fire or in a tin oven that consisted of a spit and a reflector to concentrate the heat. Cooks had to take into consideration the temperature of the fire and the temperature of the air when determining the roasting time.

Today, whether your oven is gas or electric, it has a thermostat that allows the temperature to rise to slightly above the temperature you have selected. Then the oven turns off the heat source and allows the heat to drop to slightly below your selected temperature before turning back on again. Here are some tips to keep your oven operating smoothly.

Even does it. Always preheat your oven, then check the temperature in various parts with an oven thermometer to see that it's heating evenly. Your oven should average the temperature you selected and have no hot spots that might cause burning.

Prevent smoking. Occasional cleanup is essential to keep your oven working well, particularly after roasting meats that are high in fat or whenever juices have spilled. Splashes are easiest to clean as soon as the oven is cool enough to touch and should definitely be removed before using the oven again. Otherwise they will bake on and be harder to clean. If you have a self-cleaning oven, wipe off spots just after they occur because baked-on residue will produce smoke when exposed to the high heat of cleaning.

EQUIPMENT CHECK

You probably have pans and racks suitable for roasting in your kitchen right now. But if you want to purchase new or add to your collection or just be sure you're fully equipped for success, here's what we suggest:

Heavy pans, such as stainless-steel, enameled cast-iron, or anodized aluminum roasters, or Dutch ovens—are a necessity. They will distribute the heat evenly and are less likely to warp. Plus they are strong enough to lift from the oven without spilling any juices that might have collected. **Low sides** aid evaporation and are good for crisping the bottom of foods that are being roasted on a rack. Pans with high sides prevent spattering and are good for poultry and meats that will produce a lot of drippings.

Sturdy handles are a necessity because they make it possible to remove the pan from the oven without getting your fingers or potholders into the hot and possibly slippery interior of the pan.

Roasting racks to fit each of your roasting pans.

Kitchen timer to remind you to check for doneness.

Spatulas and tongs to remove foods from the pan.

Large, heatproof board or several trivets to protect surfaces from hot roasting pans.

Good-quality potholders to protect your hands when removing hot, heavy roasting pans from the oven.

Oven thermometer to alert you if the oven needs to be recalibrated. We suggest you keep one in your oven at all times. It will help you understand the heat-flow patterns in your oven.

Meat thermometer to see if food is cooked to doneness. This is important not just for flavor but for safety. Underdone meat and poultry can harbor harmful bacteria. There are two types of meat thermometer: a heat-safe thermometer that can be inserted in the food when it goes into the oven and left there during roasting; or the newer instant-read thermometer that is inserted into the food for just a minute or two and removed after it registers the internal temperature. If you are roasting something that is just an inch or so thick, you can use a short-stemmed, instant-read "button" thermometer to check for doneness.

ROAST IT RIGHT!

Although each recipe in this book offers detailed roasting instructions, here are some tips that will make it easier to roast just about anything.

Preheat fully. Allow 10 to 15 minutes for your oven to reach the desired temperature before putting the food in.

Measure accurately. Use glass cups with spouts for liquid and metal or plastic cups with flat tops for easy leveling of dry ingredients. Standard measuring spoons are for liquid & dry measurements.

Rely on racks. Racks keep meats and poultry from simmering in their own drippings and help to brown the bottom of the roast.

Hold the lid. A roaster with a lid steams the food being roasted rather than cooking it by dry heat. This is good for poultry and tough cuts of meat but will toughen well-marbled, tender cuts of meat. Our recipes specify when you need to use a lid; otherwise, don't use one.

Roast in the center of the oven, unless instructed otherwise. Roasting on an upper rack enhances browning on the top surfaces and roasting on a lower rack increases browning on the bottom. If your roast needs additional browning on either the top or bottom, move it accordingly.

Baste as directed. Basting helps keep a roast moist and increases the flavor of the crisp outer surfaces. Some recipes use the juices that have collected in the roasting pan; others may use a marinade or broth to add extra flavor or seasonings.

Baste fish as well as other foods that dry out easily. This keeps the outer layers moist until the center is sufficiently cooked.

Boil or discard marinades and basting broths if they have been used on raw meat, poultry, or fish. These ingredients can carry bacteria. After you have finished basting raw foods you should either boil the marinade for 2 minutes to use as a sauce for the cooked food or discard it. The brush you use to coat raw food can also contaminate the basting liquid so wash it in hot soapy water before reuse. Use a clean brush or bulb baster to baste food as it roasts.

Allow meats to stand, tented with aluminum foil, for about 10 minutes after cooking. This allows the juices to redistribute evenly and helps to prevent excess moisture loss when the roast is carved.

CHICKEN & CORNISH HENS

Honey-Mustard Chicken & Potatoes

Roast Capon with Baby Carrots

Orange butter and bay leaves season this tender, juicy roast. If you can't order a capon from your supermarket, substitute a roasting chicken.

PREP: 20 MINUTES   ROAST: 2 HOURS 30 MINUTES
MAKES 10 MAIN-DISH SERVINGS.

2 navel oranges
1 capon (8 pounds)
3 tablespoons butter or
   margarine, softened
6 bay leaves
1 1/2 teaspoons salt
3/4 teaspoon coarsely ground
   black pepper

4 bunches (about 8 ounces each)
   baby carrots, peeled or 2 packages
   (16 ounces each) peeled
   baby carrots
1 cup chicken broth

1. Preheat oven to 350°F. From 1 orange, grate 1 tablespoon peel and squeeze 1/2 cup juice. Cut remaining orange into 6 wedges; set aside juice and wedges.

2. Remove giblets and neck from capon; refrigerate for another use. Rinse capon inside and out with cold running water; drain. Pat capon dry with paper towels.

3. In cup, blend butter with orange peel. With fingertips, gently separate skin from meat on capon breast and thighs. Rub butter mixture on meat under skin. Place 1 bay leaf under skin of each breast half and 1 bay leaf under skin of each thigh. Place orange wedges and remaining 2 bay leaves inside cavity of capon. Sprinkle outside of capon with 1 teaspoon salt and 1/2 teaspoon pepper.

4. With capon breast side up, lift wings up toward neck, then fold wing tips under back of capon so wings stay in place. Tie capon's legs together with string. Place capon, breast side up, on rack in medium roasting pan (14" by 10").

5. Roast capon, occasionally basting with pan drippings. After capon has cooked 1 hour 30 minutes, spoon 3 tablespoons drippings from capon into 15 1/2" by 10 1/2" jelly-roll pan. Add carrots; toss to coat. Sprinkle carrots with remaining 1/2 teaspoon salt and 1/4 teaspoon pepper. Place the carrots in oven with capon and roast, stirring once, until carrots are tender, about 1 hour. Capon is done when temperature on meat ther-

mometer inserted in thickest part of thigh, next to body, reaches 175° to 180°F and juices run clear when thigh is pierced with tip of knife.

6. Transfer capon to warm large platter; let stand 15 minutes to set juices for easier carving. Keep carrots warm.

7. Meanwhile, remove rack from roasting pan. Skim and discard fat from drippings in pan. Add broth and orange juice to pan; heat to boiling over medium-high heat. Cook 2 minutes, stirring until browned bits are loosened from bottom of pan. Place carrots on platter with capon. Serve capon and carrots with pan juices. Remove bay leaves before eating.

Each serving: About 465 calories, 47g protein, 9g carbohydrate, 26g total fat (9g saturated), 148mg cholesterol, 594mg sodium.

Roast Capon with Baby Carrots

Asian Sesame Chicken

Intense, exotic sesame oil, made from roasted sesame seeds, takes chicken from ordinary to out-of-this-world.

PREP: 15 MINUTES   ROAST: 1 HOUR   MAKES 4 MAIN-DISH SERVINGS.

1 chicken (3 1/2 pounds)
2 green onions, trimmed and minced
1 tablespoon minced, peeled
  fresh ginger
1 garlic clove, minced

2 tablespoons Asian sesame oil
1/2 teaspoon salt
1/4 teaspoon coarsely ground
  black pepper

1. Preheat oven to 450°F. Remove giblets and neck from chicken; refrigerate for another use. Rinse chicken inside and out with cold running water; drain. Pat dry with paper towels.

2. In small bowl, stir green onions, ginger, garlic, and 1 tablespoon sesame oil until mixed. With fingertips, gently separate skin from meat on chicken breast and thighs. Rub green-onion mixture on meat under skin.

3. With chicken breast side up, lift wings up toward neck, then fold wing tips under back of chicken so wings stay in place. Tie legs together with string. Sprinkle chicken with salt and pepper. Place chicken, breast side up, on rack in medium roasting pan (14" by 10").

4. Roast chicken 50 minutes. Brush with remaining 1 tablespoon sesame oil and roast about 10 minutes longer. Chicken is done when temperature on meat thermometer inserted in thickest part of the thigh, next to body, reaches 175° to 180°F and juices run clear when thickest part of thigh is pierced with tip of knife.

5. Transfer chicken to warm platter; let stand 10 minutes to set juices for easier carving.

Each serving: About 485 calories, 48g protein, 1g carbohydrate, 31g total fat (8g saturated), 154mg cholesterol, 435mg sodium.

Caribbean Chicken

To bring a taste of the tropics to your table, whip up this simple jerk seasoning in your blender.

PREP: 15 MINUTES   ROAST: 1 HOUR   MAKES 4 MAIN-DISH SERVINGS.

1 chicken (3½ pounds)	1 tablespoon chopped, peeled
2 green onions, trimmed and	fresh ginger
coarsely chopped	1 teaspoon ground allspice
2 tablespoons white wine vinegar	1 teaspoon dried thyme
2 tablespoons Worcestershire sauce	¾ teaspoon salt
1 jalapeño chile, seeded and	
coarsely chopped	

1. Preheat oven to 450°F. Remove giblets and neck from chicken; refrigerate for another use. Rinse chicken inside and out with cold running water; drain. Pat dry with paper towels.

2. In blender, combine green onions, vinegar, Worcestershire, jalapeño, ginger, allspice, thyme, and salt; puree until smooth. With fingertips, gently separate skin from meat on chicken breast and thighs. Spread half of green-onion mixture on meat under skin (mixture will be thin).

3. With chicken breast side up, lift wings up toward neck, then fold wing tips under back of chicken so wings stay in place. Tie chicken legs together with string. Place chicken, breast side up, on rack in medium roasting pan (14" by 10").

4. Roast chicken 40 minutes. Brush remaining green-onion mixture on skin; roast about 15 minutes longer. Chicken is done when temperature on meat thermometer inserted in the thickest part of thigh, next to body, reaches 175° to 180°F and juices run clear when thigh is pierced with tip of knife.

5. Transfer chicken to warm platter; let stand 10 minutes to set juices for easier carving.

Each serving: About 435 calories, 48g protein, 3g carbohydrate, 24g total fat (7g saturated), 154mg cholesterol, 665mg sodium.

Chicken Paprikash

Lots of thinly sliced onions are tossed with paprika and roasted in the pan with the chicken until they're soft and tender. Just a bit of sour cream adds a rich finish.

PREP: 15 MINUTES   ROAST: 1 HOUR   MAKES 4 MAIN-DISH SERVINGS.

1 chicken (3 1/2 pounds)
1 tablespoon butter or margarine,
   softened
1 garlic clove, crushed with
   garlic press
2 large onions (about 12 ounces
   each), thinly sliced

1 tablespoon paprika
1/2 teaspoon salt
1/4 cup water
1/4 cup chicken broth
2 tablespoons sour cream

1. Preheat oven to 450°F. Remove giblets and neck from chicken; refrigerate for another use. Rinse chicken inside and out with cold running water; drain. Pat dry with paper towels.

2. In cup, mix butter with garlic. With fingertips, gently separate skin from meat on chicken breast and thighs. Spread garlic mixture on meat under the skin.

3. With breast side up, lift wings up toward neck, then fold wing tips under back of chicken so wings stay in place. Tie legs together with string.

4. In medium roasting pan (14" by 10"), stir onions, paprika, salt, and water. Place chicken, breast side up, in pan.

5. Roast chicken, stirring onions halfway through roasting time, about 1 hour. Chicken is done when temperature on meat thermometer inserted in thickest part of thigh, next to body, reaches 175° to 180°F and juices run clear when thigh is pierced with tip of knife.

6. Transfer chicken to warm platter; let stand 10 minutes to allow juices to set for easier carving.

7. Meanwhile, skim and discard fat from onion mixture in pan. Add broth to onion mixture; heat to boiling over medium heat, stirring until browned bits are loosened from bottom of pan. Stir in sour cream. Serve chicken with onion mixture.

Each serving: About 590 calories, 50g protein, 16g carbohydrate, 35g total fat (11g saturated), 171mg cholesterol, 531mg sodium.

Mahogany Roast Chicken

Give your roast chicken a deep amber glaze by brushing it with a simple mix of balsamic vinegar, brown sugar, and dry vermouth.

PREP: 10 MINUTES   ROAST: 1 HOUR 15 MINUTES
MAKES 4 MAIN-DISH SERVINGS.

1 chicken (3 1/2 pounds)	2 tablespoons dark brown sugar
3/4 teaspoon salt	2 tablespoons balsamic vinegar
1/2 teaspoon coarsely ground	2 tablespoons dry vermouth
black pepper	1/4 cup water

1. Preheat oven to 375°F. Remove giblets and neck from chicken; reserve for another use. Rinse chicken inside and out with cold running water; drain. Pat dry with paper towels. Sprinkle salt and pepper on outside of the chicken.

2. With chicken breast side up, lift wings up toward neck, then fold wing tips under back of chicken so wings stay in place. Tie legs together with string. Place chicken, breast side up, on rack in small roasting pan (13" by 9"). Roast chicken 45 minutes.

3. Meanwhile, prepare glaze: In small bowl, stir brown sugar, vinegar, and vermouth until sugar has dissolved.

4. After chicken has roasted 45 minutes, brush with some glaze. Turn oven control to 400°F and roast chicken, brushing with glaze twice more during roasting, until chicken is deep brown, about 30 minutes longer. Chicken is done when temperature on meat thermometer inserted in thickest part of thigh, next to body, reaches 175° to 180°F and juices run clear when thigh is pierced with tip of knife.

5. Transfer chicken to warm platter; let stand 10 minutes to set juices for easier carving.

6. Meanwhile, remove rack from roasting pan. Skim and discard fat from drippings in pan. Add water to pan; heat to boiling over medium heat, stirring until browned bits are loosened from bottom of pan. Serve chicken with pan juices.

Each serving: About 446 calories, 48g protein, 7g carbohydrate, 24g total fat (7g saturated), 154mg cholesterol, 583mg sodium.

Mexico City Roast Chicken

The contrast of warm spices and brown sugar with smoky chipotle chiles in adobo adds a delicious depth of flavor.

PREP: 15 MINUTES   ROAST: 1 HOUR   MAKES 4 MAIN-DISH SERVINGS.

1 chicken (3 1/2 pounds)
2 tablespoons chipotle chiles
   in adobo (see Tip page 21),
   finely chopped
1 tablespoon brown sugar
1 tablespoon chili powder
1 tablespoon cider vinegar
1 teaspoon ground cumin
2 teaspoons tomato paste
1/2 teaspoon salt

1/8 teaspoon ground cinnamon
2 large onions (about 12 ounces
   each), each cut into 8 wedges
2 teaspoons vegetable oil
1/4 cup water
Optional accompaniments: warm flour
   tortillas, shredded lettuce, cilantro
   leaves, and lime wedges

1. Preheat oven to 450°F. Remove giblets and neck from chicken; refrigerate for another use. Rinse chicken inside and out with cold running water; drain well. Pat dry with paper towels.

2. In small bowl, combine chipotle chiles, brown sugar, chili powder, vinegar, cumin, tomato paste, salt, and cinnamon until blended (mixture will be thick). With fingertips, gently separate skin from meat on chicken breast and thighs. Spread chipotle mixture on meat under skin.

3. With chicken breast side up, lift wings up toward neck, then fold wing tips under back of chicken so wings stay in place. Tie chicken legs together with string.

4. In medium roasting pan (14" by 10"), stir onions with oil and water. Place chicken, breast side up, in pan.

5. Roast chicken, stirring onions halfway through cooking time, about 1 hour. Chicken is done when temperature on meat thermometer, inserted in thickest part of thigh, next to body, reaches 175° to 180°F and juices run clear when thigh is pierced with tip of knife.

6. Transfer chicken to warm platter; let stand 10 minutes to set juices for easier carving.

7. Meanwhile, with slotted spoon, transfer onions to platter with chicken. Skim and discard fat from drippings in pan. Serve chicken with pan juices or slice chicken and wrap in warm tortillas with lettuce and cilantro, if you like. Serve with lime wedges.

Each serving: About 590 calories, 50g protein, 21g carbohydrate, 33g total fat (9g saturated), 159mg cholesterol, 545mg sodium.

TIP
Canned chipotle chiles in adobo (smoked jalapeño chiles in a vinegary marinade) are available in Hispanic markets.

Moroccan-Style Roast Chicken

A low-stress dish for a busy weeknight. Serve with quick sides like couscous and peas.

PREP: 15 MINUTES   ROAST: 1 HOUR   MAKES 4 MAIN-DISH SERVINGS.

1 chicken (3 1/2 pounds)
1 tablespoon butter or margarine,
  softened
1 1/2 teaspoons ground cumin
1 1/2 teaspoons ground coriander
1/4 teaspoon ground cinnamon
1/4 teaspoon ground allspice
1/2 teaspoon salt

1/4 teaspoon coarsely ground
  black pepper
1 can (14 1/2 to 16 ounces)
  tomatoes, drained and
  coarsely chopped
1 tablespoon minced fresh
  cilantro leaves

1. Preheat oven to 450°F. Remove giblets and neck from chicken; refrigerate for another use. Rinse chicken inside and out with cold running water; drain well. Pat dry with paper towels.

2. In small bowl, stir butter with cumin, coriander, cinnamon, allspice, salt, and pepper until blended. With fingertips, gently separate skin from meat on breast and thighs. Rub spice mixture on meat under skin.

3. With chicken breast side up, lift wings up toward neck, then fold wing tips under back of chicken so wings stay in place. Tie chicken legs together with string. Place chicken, breast side up, on rack in medium roasting pan (14" by 10").

4. Roast chicken 40 minutes. Add tomatoes; roast about 20 minutes longer. Chicken is done when temperature on meat thermometer inserted in thickest part of thigh, next to body, reaches 175° to 180°F and juices run clear when thigh is pierced with tip of knife.

5. Transfer chicken to warm platter; let stand 10 minutes to set juices for easier carving.

6. Meanwhile, remove rack from roasting pan. Skim and discard fat from drippings in pan. Transfer tomatoes to bowl; stir in cilantro. Serve chicken with tomato mixture.

Each serving: About 470 calories, 49g protein, 5g carbohydrate, 27g total fat (8g saturated), 162mg cholesterol, 636mg sodium.

Roast Chicken Béarnaise

This classic but easy French sauce is made right in the roasting pan.

PREP: 15 MINUTES   ROAST: 1 HOUR   MAKES 4 MAIN-DISH SERVINGS.

1 chicken (3 1/2 pounds)
1 teaspoon salt
**1/2 teaspoon coarsely ground
  black pepper**
1 large lemon, cut in half
3 medium shallots
**4 sprigs fresh tarragon plus
  1 tablespoon chopped fresh
  tarragon leaves**

1/4 cup dry white wine
**1 teaspoon tarragon vinegar or white
  wine vinegar**
1 tablespoon butter or margarine

1. Preheat oven to 450°F. Remove giblets and neck from chicken; reserve for another use. Rinse chicken inside and out with cold running water; drain. Pat dry with paper towels.

2. Sprinkle 1/2 teaspoon salt and 1/4 teaspoon pepper inside cavity. Squeeze juice from lemon into cavity, then place halves inside cavity. Coarsely chop 2 shallots; add to cavity along with tarragon sprigs.

3. With chicken breast side up, lift wings up toward neck, then fold wing tips under back of chicken so wings stay in place. Tie legs together with string. Place chicken, breast side up, on rack in small roasting pan (13" by 9"). Sprinkle outside of chicken with remaining 1/2 teaspoon salt and 1/4 teaspoon pepper.

4. Roast chicken about 1 hour. Chicken is done when temperature on meat thermometer inserted in thickest part of thigh, next to body, reaches 175°F to 180°F and juices run clear when thigh is pierced with tip of knife.

5. Finely chop remaining shallot. With tongs, tilt chicken to allow juices from cavity to run into roasting pan. Transfer chicken to warm platter; let stand 10 minutes to set juices for easier carving.

6. Meanwhile, remove rack from roasting pan. Skim and discard fat from drippings in pan. Add wine, vinegar, and chopped shallot to pan; heat to boiling over high heat. Remove pan from heat; stir in butter and chopped tarragon. Serve chicken with sauce.

Each serving: About 375 calories, 40g protein, 1g carbohydrate, 22g total fat (7g saturated), 164mg cholesterol, 726mg sodium.

Peking Chicken

This succulent bird is glazed with a fragrant honey-soy sauce mixture near the end of roasting.

PREP: 20 MINUTES   ROAST: 1 HOUR   MAKES 4 MAIN-DISH SERVINGS.

1 chicken (3½ pounds)
2 tablespoons honey
2 tablespoons soy sauce
1 tablespoon minced, peeled
   fresh ginger
2 garlic cloves, crushed with
   garlic press
1 teaspoon seasoned rice vinegar
⅛ teaspoon ground red pepper
   (cayenne)

8 (8-inch) flour tortillas
¼ cup chicken broth
2 tablespoons water
¼ cup hoisin sauce
2 green onions, each cut crosswise
   into thirds, then sliced lengthwise
   into thin strips

1. Preheat oven to 450°F. Remove giblets and neck from chicken; refrigerate for another use. Rinse chicken inside and out with cold running water; drain. Pat dry with paper towels.

2. With chicken breast side up, lift wings up toward neck, then fold wing tips under back of chicken so wings stay in place. Tie legs together with string.

3. Place chicken on rack in sink. With chicken breast side up, pour *1 quart boiling water* over chicken. Turn chicken over; slowly pour an additional *1 quart boiling water* over back of chicken. (This process allows fat to render easily from chicken and helps skin get crispy during roasting.)

4. Place chicken, breast side up, on rack in small roasting pan (13" by 9"). Roast chicken 50 minutes.

5. Meanwhile, in cup, combine honey, soy sauce, ginger, garlic, vinegar, and ground red pepper; set aside.

6. After chicken has roasted 50 minutes, brush with half of honey glaze; continue roasting 5 minutes. Brush with the remaining glaze; roast about 5 minutes longer. Chicken is done when temperature on meat

thermometer inserted in thickest part of thigh, next to body, reaches 175° to 180°F and juices run clear when thigh is pierced with tip of knife.

7. Transfer chicken to warm platter; let stand 10 minutes to set juices for easier carving.

8. Meanwhile, warm tortillas as label directs. Remove rack from roasting pan. Skim and discard fat from drippings in pan. Add broth and water to pan; heat to boiling over medium heat, stirring until browned bits are loosened from bottom of pan. Stir in hoisin sauce.

9. To serve, slice chicken and wrap in tortillas with hoisin-sauce mixture and green onions.

Each serving: About 740 calories, 55g protein, 60g carbohydrate, 29g total fat (7g saturated), 154mg cholesterol, 1,405mg sodium.

Roast Chicken with Creamy Mushroom Sauce

Perfectly cooked meat and a classic sauce you make in the same roasting pan—what could be easier?

PREP: 15 MINUTES   ROAST: 1 HOUR   MAKES 4 MAIN-DISH SERVINGS.

1 chicken (3 1/2 pounds)
1/2 teaspoon salt
1/4 teaspoon coarsely ground black pepper
1 package (8 ounces) white mushrooms, each cut into quarters
1 package (3 1/2 ounces) shiitake mushrooms, stems removed and caps cut into quarters

1 tablespoon all-purpose flour
1 1/4 cups chicken broth
2 tablespoons heavy or whipping cream
1 tablespoon chopped fresh parsley

1. Preheat oven to 450°F. Remove giblets and neck from chicken; reserve for another use. Rinse chicken inside and out with cold running water; drain. Pat dry with paper towels. Sprinkle salt and pepper on outside of chicken.

2. With chicken breast side up, lift wings up toward neck, then fold wing tips under back of chicken so wings stay in place. Tie legs together with string. Place chicken, breast side up, on rack in medium roasting pan (about 14" by 10").

3. Roast chicken 15 minutes; add white and shitake mushrooms to roasting pan. Roast chicken and mushrooms about 45 minutes longer. Chicken is done when temperature on meat thermometer inserted in thickest part of thigh, next to body, reaches 175° to 180°F and juices run clear when thigh is pierced with tip of knife.

4. Transfer chicken to warm platter; let stand 10 minutes to set juices for easier carving.

5. Meanwhile, remove rack from roasting pan. Skim and discard fat from drippings in pan. In small bowl, with wire whisk, mix flour and 1/4 cup broth until smooth; stir flour mixture into mushrooms in roasting pan. Heat mushroom mixture over medium heat, stirring constantly, 1 minute. Slowly stir remaining 1 cup broth into roasting pan; cook, stirring constantly, until mixture boils and thickens slightly, about 5 minutes.

6. Remove pan from heat; stir in cream and parsley. Serve chicken with mushroom sauce.

Each serving: About 565 calories, 50g protein, 6g carbohydrate, 37g total fat (11g saturated), 172mg cholesterol, 765mg sodium.

Roast Chicken Provençal

It's cooked on a bed of red peppers and onions and seasoned with basil.

PREP: 20 MINUTES   ROAST: 1 HOUR   MAKES 4 MAIN-DISH SERVINGS.

1 chicken (3 1/2 pounds)
20 garlic cloves (1 head), loose
  papery skin discarded but
  not peeled
1/2 teaspoon salt
1/4 teaspoon coarsely ground
  black pepper
2 medium red peppers, cut into
  1 1/2-inch-wide slices

1 large onion (about 12 ounces), cut
  into 1/2-inch-wide wedges
1 teaspoon olive oil
3/4 cup water
1/2 cup Mediterranean olives, such as
  Kalamata, picholine, or Niçoise
1/2 cup chicken broth
2 tablespoons chopped fresh
  basil leaves

1. Preheat oven to 450°F. Remove giblets and neck from chicken; reserve for another use. Rinse chicken inside and out with cold running water; drain. Pat dry with paper towels.

2. Place garlic cloves inside cavity of chicken. Sprinkle outside of chicken with salt and pepper.

3. With chicken breast side up, lift wings up toward neck, then fold wing tips under back of chicken so wings stay in place. Tie chicken legs together with string.

4. Place peppers and onion in medium roasting pan (14" by 10"); stir in oil and 1/4 cup water. Place chicken, breast side up, on vegetables.

5. Roast chicken and vegetables 45 minutes. Stir olives into vegetable mixture and roast about 15 minutes longer. Chicken is done when temperature on meat thermometer inserted in thickest part of thigh, next to body, reaches 175° to 180°F and juices run clear when thigh is pierced with tip of knife.

6. Transfer chicken to platter; let stand 10 minutes to set juices for carving.

7. Meanwhile, with slotted spoon, transfer vegetable mixture to platter with chicken. Skim and discard fat from drippings in pan. Add chicken broth, basil, and remaining 1/2 cup water to pan; heat to boiling over medium heat, stirring until browned bits are loosened from bottom of pan. Serve chicken with vegetables and pan juices.

Each serving: About 600 calories, 50g protein, 16g carbohydrate, 36g total fat (9g saturated), 159mg cholesterol, 875mg sodium.

Roast Chicken with Forty Cloves of Garlic

Serve with lots of crusty bread for spreading the luscious roasted garlic.

PREP: 15 MINUTES   ROAST: 1 HOUR   MAKES 4 MAIN-DISH SERVINGS.

1 chicken (3 1/2 pounds)
6 thyme sprigs
1/2 teaspoon salt
1/4 teaspoon coarsely ground
  black pepper

40 garlic cloves (2 heads), loose
  papery skin discarded but
  not peeled
1 cup chicken broth

1. Preheat oven to 450°F. Remove giblets and neck from chicken; reserve for another use. Rinse chicken inside and out with cold running water; drain. Pat dry with paper towels.

2. With fingertips, gently separate skin from meat on chicken breast. Place 2 thyme sprigs under skin of each breast half. Place remaining 2 sprigs inside cavity of chicken. Sprinkle salt and pepper on outside of chicken.

3. With chicken breast side up, lift wings up toward neck, then fold wing tips under back of chicken so wings stay in place. Tie legs together with string. Place, breast side up, on rack in small roasting pan (13" by 9").

4. Roast chicken 30 minutes. Add garlic cloves to pan; roast about 30 minutes longer. Chicken is done when temperature on meat thermometer inserted in thickest part of thigh, next to body, reaches 175° to 180°F and juices run clear when thigh is pierced with tip of knife.

5. Transfer chicken to platter; let stand 10 minutes to set juices for carving.

6. Meanwhile, remove rack from roasting pan. With slotted spoon, transfer garlic cloves to small bowl. Skim and discard fat from drippings in pan. Remove and discard skin from 6 garlic cloves; return peeled garlic to roasting pan and add broth. Heat broth mixture to boiling over medium heat, stirring until browned bits are loosened from bottom of pan and mashing garlic with back of spoon until well blended. Serve chicken with pan juices and remaining garlic cloves.

Each serving: About 501 calories, 50g protein, 11g carbohydrate, 28g total fat (8g saturated), 157mg cholesterol, 688mg sodium.

Roast Chicken with Green Olives and Sherry

Tangy green olives and dry sherry give this chicken Spanish flair.

PREP: 15 MINUTES   ROAST: 1 HOUR   MAKES 4 MAIN-DISH SERVINGS.

1 chicken (3 1/2 pounds)
12 green olives, such as manzanilla, pitted and finely chopped
1 tablespoon chopped fresh parsley
1 small shallot, minced
1 garlic clove, minced
1/2 teaspoon freshly grated lemon peel

1 tablespoon extravirgin olive oil
1/4 teaspoon salt
1/4 teaspoon coarsely ground black pepper
3/4 cup chicken broth
3 tablespoons dry sherry

1. Preheat oven to 450°F. Remove giblets and neck from chicken; reserve for another use. Rinse chicken inside and out with cold running water; drain. Pat dry with paper towels.

2. In small bowl, combine olives, parsley, shallot, garlic, lemon peel, oil, salt, and pepper until well blended. With fingertips, gently separate skin from meat on chicken breast and thighs. Rub olive mixture on meat under skin.

3. With chicken breast side up, lift wings up toward neck, then fold wing tips under back of chicken so wings stay in place. Tie legs together with string. Place, breast side up, on rack in small roasting pan (13" by 9").

4. Roast chicken about 1 hour. Chicken is done when temperature on meat thermometer inserted in thickest part of thigh, next to body, reaches 175° to 180°F and juices run clear when chicken thigh is pierced with tip of knife.

5. Transfer chicken to platter; let stand 10 minutes to set juices for carving.

6. Meanwhile, remove rack from roasting pan. Skim and discard fat from drippings in pan. Add broth and sherry to pan; heat to boiling over medium heat, stirring until browned bits are loosened from bottom of pan. Serve chicken with pan-juice mixture.

Each serving: About 494 calories, 48g protein, 2g carbohydrate, 30g total fat (7g saturated), 154mg cholesterol, 712mg sodium.

Roast Chicken with Orange Peel and Bay Leaves

When grating the peel for this simple orange butter, avoid grating any of the bitter white pith.

PREP: 10 MINUTES   ROAST: 1 HOUR   MAKES 4 MAIN-DISH SERVINGS.

1 chicken (3 1/2 pounds)
2 tablespoons butter or
   margarine, softened
1 1/2 teaspoons finely grated
   orange peel

1/2 teaspoon salt
1/4 teaspoon coarsely ground
   black pepper
6 bay leaves

1. Preheat oven to 450°F. Remove giblets and neck from chicken; reserve for another use. Rinse chicken inside and out with cold running water; drain. Pat dry with paper towels.

2. In small bowl, stir butter with orange peel, 1/4 teaspoon salt, and pepper until blended. With fingertips, gently separate skin from meat on chicken breast and thighs. Rub butter mixture on meat under skin. Place 1 bay leaf under skin of each breast half. Place remaining 4 bay leaves inside cavity of chicken. Sprinkle outside of chicken with remaining 1/4 teaspoon salt.

3. With breast side up, lift wings up toward neck, then fold wing tips under back of chicken so wings stay in place. Tie chicken legs together with string. Place chicken, breast side up, on rack in small roasting pan (13" by 9").

4. Roast chicken about 1 hour. Chicken is done when temperature on meat thermometer inserted in thickest part of thigh, next to body, reaches 175° to 180°F and juices run clear when chicken thigh is pierced with tip of knife.

5. Transfer chicken to warm platter; let stand 10 minutes to set juices for easier carving. Discard bay leaves.

Each serving: About 475 calories, 48g protein, 1g carbohydrate, 30g total fat (11g saturated), 170mg cholesterol, 482mg sodium.

Roast Chicken with Sweet Potatoes

Roasting a whole chicken with sweet potatoes, onion, and an apple means deliciously flavored accompaniments are ready when the chicken is. If you use a larger pan, the vegetables may brown more quickly, so check and remove them when they are tender.

PREP: 10 MINUTES   ROAST: 1 HOUR   MAKES 4 MAIN-DISH SERVINGS.

1 chicken (3 1/2 pounds)
2 medium sweet potatoes (about 10 ounces each), unpeeled and each cut into 8 wedges
1 jumbo spring or sweet onion (1 pound), cut into 8 wedges

3/4 teaspoon salt
1/4 teaspoon freshly ground pepper
1 Golden Delicious apple, unpeeled, cored, and cut into 8 wedges
2 tablespoons orange marmalade

1. Preheat oven to 450°F. Remove giblets and neck from chicken; reserve for another use.

2. With chicken breast side up, lift wings up toward neck, then fold wing tips under back of chicken so wings stay in place. Tie legs together with string.

3. Place chicken, breast side up, on rack in medium roasting pan (14" by 10"). Place sweet-potato and onion wedges around rack in pan. Rub 1/2 teaspoon salt and 1/4 teaspoon pepper on outside of chicken. Sprinkle vegetables with remaining 1/4 teaspoon salt. Roast chicken and vegetables 40 minutes. Remove pan from oven; tilt chicken to drain juices from cavity onto vegetables. Add apple wedges to pan.

4. Return pan with chicken, vegetables, and apple wedges to oven; roast 15 minutes longer. Brush chicken with marmalade; roast until vegetables and apples are tender, about 5 minutes longer. Chicken is done when temperature on meat thermometer inserted into thickest part of thigh, next to body, reaches 175° to 180°F and juices run clear when thigh is pierced with tip of knife.

5. Transfer chicken to warm large platter; spoon vegetable mixture around chicken. Remove skin from chicken before eating, if you like.

Each serving without skin: About 470 calories, 39g protein, 47g carbohydrate, 15g total fat (4g saturated), 113mg cholesterol, 535mg sodium.

Roast Chicken with Sweet Potatoes

Roast Chicken with Pears & Sage

If you can't get fresh sage, used dried whole-leaf sage. Crumble 1 teaspoon of the leaves mix with the butter; use 6 whole leaves in the chicken cavity.

PREP: 15 MINUTES   ROAST: 1 HOUR   MAKES 4 MAIN-DISH SERVINGS.

1 chicken (3 1/2 pounds)
1 teaspoon thinly sliced fresh sage
  leaves plus 6 sprigs
1/4 teaspoon coarsely ground
  black pepper
2 tablespoons plus 1 teaspoon butter
  or margarine, softened

1/2 teaspoon salt
1 medium red onion, cut into
  1/2-inch-thick slices
1/4 cup water
2 medium Bosc or Anjou pears,
  peeled, cored, and each cut
  into quarters

1. Preheat oven to 450°F. Remove giblets and neck from chicken; reserve for another use. Rinse chicken inside and out with cold running water; drain. Pat dry with paper towels.

2. In small bowl, stir sliced sage, pepper, 2 tablespoons butter, and 1/4 teaspoon salt. With fingertips, gently separate skin from meat on breast and thighs. Rub herb mixture on meat under skin. Place sage sprigs inside cavity of chicken. Sprinkle outside of chicken with remaining 1/4 teaspoon salt.

3. With breast side up, lift wings up toward neck, then fold wing tips under back of chicken so wings stay in place. Tie legs together with string.

4. In small roasting pan (13" by 9"), melt remaining 1 teaspoon butter in oven. Remove pan from oven; stir in onion and water. Place chicken, breast side up, on rack in roasting pan with onion. Roast chicken 30 minutes. Add pears and roast 30 minutes longer. Chicken is done when meat thermometer inserted in thickest part of thigh, next to body, reaches 175° to 180°F and juices run clear when thigh is pierced with tip of knife.

5. Transfer chicken to warm platter; let stand 10 minutes to set juices for easier carving.

6. Meanwhile, remove rack from pan. Skim and discard fat from pear mixture. Transfer pear mixture to platter with chicken.

Each serving: About 600 calories, 49g protein, 17g carbohydrate, 37g total fat (13g saturated), 176mg cholesterol, 497mg sodium.

Tandoori-Style Chicken

A low-fat yogurt coating spiked with lime juice and spices adds zip to skinless chicken.

PREP: 15 MINUTES   ROAST: 1 HOUR   MAKES 4 MAIN-DISH SERVINGS.

1 chicken (3 1/2 pounds),
  skin removed
1 container (8 ounces) plain
  lowfat yogurt
1/2 small onion, chopped
1 tablespoon paprika
2 tablespoons fresh lime juice
1 tablespoon minced, peeled
  fresh ginger

1 teaspoon ground cumin
1 teaspoon ground coriander
3/4 teaspoon salt
1/4 teaspoon ground red pepper
  (cayenne)
pinch ground cloves

1. Preheat oven to 450°F. Remove giblets and neck from chicken; reserve for another use. Rinse chicken inside and out with cold running water; drain well. Pat dry with paper towels.

2. With chicken breast side up, lift wings up toward neck, then fold wing tips under back of chicken so wings stay in place. Tie chicken legs together with string.

3. In blender, combine yogurt, onion, paprika, lime juice, ginger, cumin, coriander, salt, ground red pepper, and cloves, and puree until smooth.

4. Place chicken in large bowl. Coat chicken inside and out with yogurt mixture. Place chicken, breast side up, on rack in small roasting pan (13" by 9"). Brush outside of chicken with half of yogurt mixture remaining in bowl; reserve any remaining mixture.

5. Roast chicken 30 minutes. Brush chicken with remaining yogurt mixture; roast about 30 minutes longer. Chicken is done when meat thermometer inserted into thickest part of thigh, next to body, reaches 175° to 180°F and juices run clear when thigh is pierced with tip of knife.

6. Transfer chicken to warm platter; let stand 10 minutes to set juices for easier carving.

Each serving: About 320 calories, 45g protein, 7g carbohydrate, 12g total fat (4g saturated), 130mg cholesterol, 600mg sodium.

Lemon-Roasted Chicken for a Crowd

When you need a special dish for a big party but don't have time to fuss, turn to this crowd-pleasing recipe.

PREP: 20 MINUTES   ROAST: 1 HOUR 30 MINUTES
MAKES 20 MAIN-DISH SERVINGS.

1½ cups fresh lemon juice (7 large lemons)
¼ cup vegetable oil
1 large onion (12 ounces), finely chopped
2 large garlic cloves, crushed with garlic press

1 tablespoon plus 2 teaspoons salt
1 tablespoon dried thyme
2 teaspoons ground black pepper
5 chickens (3 pounds each), each cut into quarters

1. Preheat oven to 375°F. In medium bowl, combine lemon juice, oil, onion, garlic, salt, thyme, and pepper. In two large roasting pans (17" by 11½"), arrange chicken, skin side up. Pour the lemon-juice mixture over the chicken.

2. Roast chicken, basting occasionally with pan juices, until juices run clear when thickest part of chicken is pierced with tip of knife, about 1 hour 30 minutes.

3. Transfer chicken to warm platters. Skim and discard fat from drippings in pan; pour pan juices into medium bowl. Spoon some pan juices over chicken and serve chicken with remaining juices.

Each serving: About 381 calories, 41g protein, 3g carbohydrate, 22g total fat (6g saturated), 132mg cholesterol, 706mg sodium.

Herb Chicken

The simplest dishes are often the best. Here, fresh summer herbs are all it takes to make an exquisitely flavored roast chicken.

Prep: 10 minutes Roast: 40 minutes
Makes 8 main-dish servings.

2 tablespoons chopped fresh thyme
  or 2 teaspoons dried thyme
2 tablespoons chopped fresh
  rosemary or 2 teaspoons dried
  rosemary, crumbled
1 tablespoon olive oil

2 teaspoons paprika
1½ teaspoons salt
1 teaspoon coarsely ground
  black pepper
2 chickens (3½ pounds each),
  each cut into quarters

1. Preheat oven to 425°F. In small bowl, combine chopped thyme, rosemary, oil, paprika, salt, and pepper. Rub herb mixture on chicken quarters.
2. Arrange chicken quarters, skin side up, on rack in large roasting pan (17" by 11½"). Roast chicken (do not turn) or until golden and juices run clear when thickest part of chicken is pierced with tip of knife, about 40 minutes.
3. Transfer chicken to warm large platter and serve.

Each serving: About 380 calories, 42g protein, 1g carbohydrate, 22g total fat (6g saturated), 166mg cholesterol, 520mg sodium.

Rosemary-Apricot Chicken

Served hot or cold, this succulent roast has a delicious, tangy-sweet flavor that everyone will love.

PREP: 20 MINUTES PLUS MARINATING   ROAST: 45 MINUTES
MAKES 12 MAIN-DISH SERVINGS.

4 garlic cloves, crushed with
  garlic press
2 teaspoons salt
1 teaspoon dried rosemary, crumbled
1/2 teaspoon ground black pepper
3 chickens (3 pounds each), each cut
  into quarters and skin removed
  from all but wings

1/2 cup apricot preserves
2 tablespoons fresh lemon juice
2 teaspoons Dijon mustard

1. In cup, combine garlic, salt, rosemary, and pepper; rub mixture on chicken. Place chicken in large bowl or ziptight plastic bags; cover bowl or seal bags and refrigerate chicken 2 hours to marinate.

2. Preheat oven to 350°F. Arrange chicken, skinned side up, in two large roasting pans (17" by 11 1/2") or two jelly-roll pans (15 1/2" by 10 1/2"). Roast chicken, rotating pans between upper and lower oven racks halfway through roasting, 25 minutes.

3. Meanwhile, in small bowl, with fork, mix apricot preserves, lemon juice, and mustard. Brush apricot mixture over chicken; roast until juices run clear when thickest part of chicken is pierced with tip of knife, about 20 minutes longer, rotating pans after 10 minutes.

4. Serve chicken hot, or cover and refrigerate to serve cold.

Each serving: About 267 calories, 35g protein, 9g carbohydrate, 9g total fat (2g saturated), 108mg cholesterol, 519mg sodium.

Lime Chicken

We combined sweet brown sugar and piquant lime juice to make a wonderful pan sauce for this juicy oven-roasted chicken.

PREP: 15 MINUTES   ROAST: 50 MINUTES   MAKES 4 MAIN-DISH SERVINGS.

2 small limes
1 chicken (3 1/2 pounds), cut into
    8 pieces
3 tablespoons butter or margarine
1/4 cup all-purpose flour
3/4 teaspoon salt

1/2 teaspoon ground black pepper
2 tablespoons light brown sugar
1 can (14 1/2 ounces) reduced-sodium
    chicken broth

1. Preheat oven to 400°F. From limes, grate 2 teaspoons peel and squeeze 2 tablespoons juice. In large bowl, toss chicken pieces with lime juice. In large roasting pan (17" by 11 1/2"), melt butter in oven. Remove pan from the oven.

2. On waxed paper, combine flour, salt, and pepper. Coat chicken pieces with flour mixture. Dip chicken pieces, one at a time, into melted butter in roasting pan, turning to coat. Arrange chicken pieces, skin side up, in pan. (Do not use a smaller pan and crowd the chicken pieces; they won't brown.)

3. In cup, mix grated lime peel and brown sugar; sprinkle over chicken pieces. Pour broth into pan and roast, basting chicken with pan juices occasionally, until chicken is tender and juices run clear when pierced with tip of knife, about 50 minutes.

4. Transfer chicken to 4 dinner plates. Skim fat from drippings in pan. Spoon pan juices over chicken.

Each serving: About 505 calories, 43g protein, 14g carbohydrate, 29g total fat (11g saturated), 189mg cholesterol, 623mg sodium.

Thyme Roasted Chicken & Vegetables

A tempting one-dish meal with fennel, potatoes, and onion that's ready in just over an hour.

PREP: 20 MINUTES   BAKE: 50 MINUTES   MAKES 4 MAIN-DISH SERVINGS.

1 chicken (3 1/2 pounds) cut into
  8 pieces and skin removed from
  all but wings
1 pound all-purpose potatoes
  (3 medium), not peeled, cut into
  2-inch pieces
1 large fennel bulb (about
  1 1/2 pounds), trimmed and
  cut into 8 wedges

1 large red onion, cut into 8 wedges
2 tablespoons olive oil
1 tablespoon chopped fresh thyme or
  1 teaspoon dried thyme
1 teaspoon salt
1/2 teaspoon ground black pepper
1/3 cup hot water

1. Preheat oven to 450°F. In large roasting pan (17" by 11 1/2"), arrange chicken pieces, skinned side up, and place potatoes, fennel, and onion around it. Sprinkle chicken with thyme, salt, and pepper. Drizzle oil over chicken and vegetables.

2. Roast chicken and vegetables, basting with drippings in pan, 20 minutes. Roast, basting once more, until juices run clear when chicken breasts are pierced with tip of knife, about 20 minutes longer. Transfer chicken breasts to platter; keep warm.

3. Continue roasting remaining chicken pieces until juices run clear when thickest part of chicken is pierced with tip of knife and the vegetables are fork tender, about 10 minutes longer. Transfer chicken and vegetables to platter with breasts; keep warm.

4. To drippings, add water; heat to boiling over high heat, stirring until browned bits are loosened from bottom of pan. Spoon pan juices over chicken and vegetables.

Each serving: About 401 calories, 43g protein, 28g carbohydrate, 13g total fat (2g saturated), 124mg cholesterol, 870mg sodium.

Thyme Roasted Chicken & Vegetables

Roast Chicken with Mushrooms & Peas

The addition of sweet peas and earthy mushrooms livens up simple roast chicken pieces.

Prep: 15 minutes   Roast: 35 to 40 minutes
Makes 4 main-dish servings.

1 chicken (3 1/2 pounds), cut into
   8 pieces
8 ounces cremini or white
   mushrooms, trimmed and each cut
   into quarters
2 small onions, each cut into
   6 wedges

1 teaspoon dried thyme
1 tablespoon olive oil
1 teaspoon salt
1/2 teaspoon coarsely ground
   black pepper
1 cup frozen peas, thawed
1/4 cup hot water (optional)

1. Preheat oven to 450°F. Arrange chicken skin side up in large roasting pan (17" by 11 1/2") or jelly-roll pan (15 1/2" by 10 1/2"). Add mushrooms, onion wedges, and thyme to pan with chicken. Sprinkle with salt and pepper. Drizzle with oil.

2. Roast chicken and vegetables until juices run clear when thickest part of chicken is pierced with tip of knife, 35 to 40 minutes. Add peas and heat through. Transfer chicken and vegetables to platter; keep warm.

3. If you like, skim and discard fat from drippings in pan, then add water to pan, stirring until browned bits are loosened from bottom of pan. Spoon pan juices over chicken and vegetables.

Each serving: About 465 calories, 42g protein, 12g carbohydrate, 27g total fat (7g saturated), 156mg cholesterol, 685mg sodium.

Roast Chicken with Potatoes & Garlic

Here's a satisfying cold-weather meal. Use the roasted garlic to spread on slices of crusty bread.

PREP: 15 MINUTES   ROAST: 35 TO 40 MINUTES
MAKES 4 MAIN-DISH SERVINGS.

1 chicken (3 1/2 pounds), cut into
8 pieces
1 pound small red potatoes, each
cut into quarters
1 small red pepper, cut into
1-inch pieces
1 small yellow pepper, cut into
1-inch pieces
1 whole head garlic, cloves separated
and unpeeled

1 tablespoon dried rosemary,
crumbled
1 tablespoon olive oil
1 teaspoon salt
1/2 teaspoon coarsely ground
black pepper
1/4 cup hot water (optional)

1. Preheat oven to 450°F. Arrange chicken skin side up in large roasting pan (17" by 11 1/2") or jelly-roll pan (15 1/2" by 10 1/2"). Add potatoes, peppers, garlic cloves, and rosemary to pan with chicken. Sprinkle chicken pieces and vegetables with salt and pepper. Drizzle with oil.

2. Roast chicken and vegetables until juices run clear when thickest part of chicken is pierced with tip of knife, 35 to 40 minutes. Transfer chicken and vegetables to platter; keep warm.

3. After roasting, squeeze garlic from peels, if you like.

4. If you like, skim and discard fat from drippings in pan, then add hot water to pan, stirring until browned bits are loosened from bottom of pan. Spoon pan juices over chicken and vegetables.

Each serving: About 520 calories, 42g protein, 26g carbohydrate, 27g total fat (7g saturated), 156mg cholesterol, 655mg sodium.

Roast Chicken with Squash

Roast Chicken with Squash

Sweet prunes and savory rosemary flavor this luscious low-maintenance meal. And it's packed with protein and fiber.

PREP: 25 MINUTES   ROAST: 50 MINUTES
MAKES 4 MAIN-DISH SERVINGS.

1 cup long-grain brown rice
1 chicken (3½ pounds), cut into
  8 pieces and skin removed from
  all but wings
2 large red onions (12 ounces each),
  each cut into 8 wedges
1 acorn squash (about 2 pounds),
  seeded and cut into 8 wedges
2 tablespoons olive oil

2 tablespoons chopped fresh
  rosemary or 1 teaspoon dried
  rosemary, crumbled
1 tablespoon freshly grated
  lemon peel
1½ teaspoons salt
½ teaspoon coarsely ground
  black pepper
1 cup pitted prunes, each cut in half

1. Prepare rice as label directs; keep warm.

2. Meanwhile, preheat oven to 450°F. In large roasting pan (17" by 11½"), toss chicken, onions, and squash with oil; sprinkle with rosemary, lemon peel, salt, and pepper.

3. Roast chicken and vegetables, stirring twice, until juices run clear when thickest part of chicken breast is pierced with tip of knife, about 20 minutes. Transfer chicken breasts to platter; keep warm.

4. Add prunes to roasting pan and continue roasting until juices run clear when thickest part of remaining chicken pieces is pierced with tip of knife and vegetables are tender, about 15 minutes longer. Transfer remaining chicken pieces and vegetables to platter with breasts. Serve chicken and vegetables with brown rice.

Each serving: About 650 calories, 48g protein, 81g carbohydrate, 14g total fat (3g saturated), 131mg cholesterol, 960mg sodium.

Lemony Roast Chicken with Artichokes

Cook plump thighs and drumsticks with spring artichokes and baby red potatoes for a delectable dinner. Make sure to use a large roasting pan; otherwise ingredients will steam, not brown.

PREP: 30 MINUTES   ROAST: 40 MINUTES
MAKES 6 MAIN-DISH SERVINGS.

2 large lemons
3 garlic cloves, crushed with
  garlic press
3 tablespoons olive oil
1 1/2 teaspoons salt
1 teaspoon dried oregano
1/2 teaspoon coarsely ground
  black pepper

6 medium bone-in chicken thighs
  (about 1 3/4 pounds), skin and
  fat removed
6 medium chicken drumsticks (about
  1 1/2 pounds), skin removed
2 pounds baby red potatoes, each
  cut in half
4 medium or 16 baby artichokes

1. Preheat oven to 450°F. From lemons, grate 2 teaspoons peel and squeeze 1/2 cup juice.

2. In cup, mix lemon peel with garlic, oil, salt, oregano, and pepper. In large roasting pan (17" by 11 1/2"), toss chicken thighs, drumsticks, and potatoes with oil mixture. Roast 20 minutes.

3. While chicken is roasting, prepare artichokes: With serrated knife, cut 1 inch straight across top of medium artichoke. Cut off stem; peel. Pull dark outer leaves from artichoke bottom. With kitchen shears, trim thorny tips of remaining leaves. Cut artichoke lengthwise into quarters. Scrape out choke, removing center petals and fuzzy center portion; discard. Repeat with remaining artichokes. Rinse artichokes well. To prepare baby artichokes, see Tip.

4. In 5-quart saucepot, heat 1 tablespoon lemon juice and *1 inch water* to boiling over medium-high heat. Add artichokes and stems and cook, covered, until fork-tender, about 10 minutes. Drain well on paper towels.

5. Add artichokes to roasting pan with chicken, and roast until juices run clear when thickest part of chicken is pierced with tip of knife and potatoes are tender, about 20 minutes longer.

6. Pour remaining lemon juice over chicken and vegetables; toss before serving. Transfer chicken and vegetables to serving bowl.

Each serving: About 385 calories, 34g protein, 36g carbohydrate, 12g total fat (2g saturated), 111mg cholesterol, 740mg sodium.

TIP

To prepare baby artichokes: Bend back green outer leaves and snap them off at base until remaining leaves are half green (at the top) and half yellow (at the bottom). Cut off stems and top of each artichoke at point where yellow meets green. Cut each artichoke lengthwise in half. Do not discard center portion; baby artichokes are completely edible.

Pan-Roasted Chicken & Spinach

Boneless chicken thighs, red potatoes, onion wedges, and spinach are roasted together for an easy and satisfying one-dish meal.

PREP: 15 MINUTES   ROAST: 45 MINUTES
MAKES 4 MAIN-DISH SERVINGS.

1½ pounds red potatoes, cut into
  1½-inch chunks
1 jumbo onion (1 pound), cut into
  12 wedges
4 garlic cloves, peeled
2 tablespoons olive oil
1¼ teaspoons salt

½ teaspoon ground black pepper
½ teaspoon dried rosemary
1 pound skinless, boneless chicken
  thighs, each cut into quarters
1 bag (10 ounces) spinach,
  stems discarded

1. Preheat oven to 475°F. In large roasting pan (17" by 11½"), combine potatoes, onion, garlic, oil, salt, pepper, and rosemary; toss to coat.
2. Roast vegetables, stirring once, 25 minutes. Add chicken, tossing to coat; roast until juices run clear when thickest part of chicken is pierced with tip of knife, about 15 minutes longer.
3. Place spinach over chicken mixture and roast until spinach has wilted, about 5 minutes longer. Toss before serving.

Each serving: About 440 calories, 34g protein, 48g carbohydrate, 13g total fat (2g saturated), 118mg cholesterol, 930mg sodium.

Pan-Roasted Chicken & Spinach

Honey-Mustard Chicken & Potatoes

Honey-Mustard Chicken & Potatoes

It all cooks in the oven at the same time. Delicious with steamed fresh green beans.

PREP: 10 MINUTES   ROAST: 50 MINUTES   MAKES 4 MAIN-DISH SERVINGS.

1¹/₂ pounds small red potatoes, each cut into quarters

1 jumbo onion (1 pound), cut into eighths

6 teaspoons olive oil

³/₄ teaspoon salt

¹/₄ teaspoon coarsely ground black pepper

4 medium chicken breast halves, skin removed

2 tablespoons honey mustard

1. Preheat oven to 450°F. In small roasting pan (13" by 9"), toss potatoes and onion with 4 teaspoons oil, salt, and pepper. Place pan on middle rack and roast 25 minutes.

2. Meanwhile, place chicken breast halves in separate small roasting pan (13" by 9"); coat chicken with 1 teaspoon oil. In cup, mix remaining 1 teaspoon oil with honey mustard; set aside.

3. After vegetables have baked 25 minutes, remove pan from oven and carefully turn vegetables with metal spatula. Return vegetables to oven, placing pan on lower oven rack. Place chicken on upper rack.

4. After chicken has baked 10 minutes, remove from oven; brush with honey-mustard mixture. Bake chicken and vegetables 12 to 15 minutes longer, until juices run clear when thickest part of chicken is pierced with a knife and vegetables are golden and tender. Serve chicken with vegetables.

Each serving: About 380 calories, 31g protein, 44g carbohydrate, 10g total fat (1g saturated), 66mg cholesterol, 630mg sodium.

Roasted Tandoori-Style Chicken Breasts

In this favorite Indian dish, plain yogurt tenderizes the chicken, while the exotic spices add lots of flavor.

PREP: 10 MINUTES PLUS MARINATING   ROAST: 30 MINUTES
MAKES 6 MAIN-DISH SERVINGS.

2 limes
1 container (8 ounces) plain
   lowfat yogurt
1/2 small onion, chopped
1 tablespoon minced, peeled
   fresh ginger
1 tablespoon paprika
1 teaspoon ground cumin

1 teaspoon ground coriander
3/4 teaspoon salt
1/4 teaspoon ground red pepper
   (cayenne)
pinch ground cloves
6 medium bone-in chicken breast
   halves (3 pounds), skin removed

1. From 1 lime, squeeze 2 tablespoons juice. Cut the remaining lime into 6 wedges; set aside.

2. In blender, combine lime juice, yogurt, onion, ginger, paprika, cumin, coriander, salt, ground red pepper, and cloves; puree until smooth. Place chicken and yogurt marinade in medium bowl or in ziptight plastic bag, turning to coat chicken. Cover bowl or seal bag and refrigerate chicken 30 minutes to marinate.

3. Preheat oven to 450°F. Arrange chicken on rack in medium roasting pan (14" by 10"). Spoon half of the marinade over chicken; discard the remaining marinade.

4. Roast chicken until juices run clear when thickest part of chicken is pierced with tip of knife, about 30 minutes.

5. Transfer chicken to warm platter and serve with lime wedges.

Each serving: About 197 calories, 36g protein, 5g carbohydrate, 3g total fat (1g saturated), 88mg cholesterol, 415mg sodium.

Citrus-Glazed Cornish Hens

This delicious dish is done in just 30 minutes! Simply blend lemon juice, marmalade, and soy sauce and warm over low heat, then brush the glaze over the hens and roast.

PREP: 10 MINUTES   ROAST: 20 MINUTES
MAKES 4 MAIN-DISH SERVINGS.

2 refrigerated pre-roasted Cornish
  hens (1¼ pounds each), each cut
  lengthwise in half (see Tip below)

1 small lemon
¼ cup orange marmalade
2 teaspoons soy sauce

1. Preheat oven to 450°F. Place hens, skin side up, in large roasting pan (17" by 11½"). Roast hens 20 minutes.

2. Meanwhile, grate 1 teaspoon peel and squeeze 1 tablespoon juice from lemon. In 1-quart saucepan, heat lemon peel, lemon juice, orange marmalade, and soy sauce over low heat until marmalade melts.

3. Brush hen halves with marmalade mixture frequently during last 10 minutes of roasting time.

4. Skim and discard fat from drippings in pan. Serve hens with pan juices.

Each serving: About 460 calories, 35g protein, 15g carbohydrate, 28g total fat (8g saturated), 203mg cholesterol, 275mg sodium.

TIP

Cornish hens can be cut in half before or after cooking. It's easiest to use poultry shears, but a large knife will also work well. Place hen, breast side up, on cutting board. Slit closely along breastbone with a knife to loosen the meat. Cut along one side of the breastbone with shears. Turn bird breast side down; cut along each side of backbone and discard it.

Cornish Hens Milanese

Italians call the mix of lemon peel, garlic, and parsley *gremolata*.

PREP: 5 MINUTES   ROAST: 50 MINUTES   MAKES 4 MAIN-DISH SERVINGS.

2 Cornish hens (1 1/2 pounds each)
3 tablespoons chopped fresh parsley
1 teaspoon extravirgin olive oil
1/4 teaspoon salt

1/8 teaspoon ground black pepper
1 small garlic clove, minced
1/2 teaspoon freshly grated lemon peel

1. Preheat oven to 375°F. Remove giblets and necks from hens; reserve for another use. With poultry shears, cut each hen lengthwise in half (see Tip page 53). Rinse hen halves with cold running water; pat dry with paper towels.

2. In small bowl, combine 2 tablespoons parsley, oil, salt, and pepper. With fingertips, carefully separate skin from meat on each hen half; spread parsley mixture under skin. Place the hens, skin side up, in large roasting pan (17" by 11 1/2").

3. Roast hens, basting with drippings three times, until juices run clear when thickest part of thigh is pierced with tip of knife, about 50 minutes.

4. Transfer hens to warm platter. In cup, combine remaining 1 tablespoon parsley, garlic, and lemon peel; sprinkle over hens.

Each serving: About 384 calories, 32g protein, 0g carbohydrate, 27g total fat (7g saturated), 187mg cholesterol, 236mg sodium.

Cornish Hens Milanese

Cornish Hens with Acorn Squash

This simple but hearty dish is made with apple cider—perfect for a cool autumn evening.

PREP: 20 MINUTES ROAST: 1 HOUR 15 MINUTES
MAKES 6 MAIN-DISH SERVINGS.

3 Cornish hens (1¼ pounds each)
2 medium acorn squash (about
   1¼ pounds each)
¾ teaspoon salt
½ teaspoon coarsely ground
   black pepper

1 cup apple cider or apple juice
½ cup pitted prunes (3 ounces)
2 cinnamon sticks (3 inches each)

1. Preheat oven to 375°F. Remove giblets and necks from hens; reserve for another use. Rinse hens inside and out with cold running water; drain. Pat hens dry with paper towels.

2. Cut acorn squash lengthwise in half; remove and discard seeds. Cut each squash half lengthwise into 3 wedges, then cut each wedge diagonally in half.

3. With hens breast side up, lift wings up toward neck, then fold wing tips under back of hens so they stay in place. Tie the legs of each hen together with string.

4. Place hens, breast side up, in center of a large roasting pan (17" by 11½"); rub with salt and pepper. Arrange squash pieces in roasting pan around hens.

5. Roast hens and squash 30 minutes. Add apple cider, prunes, and cinnamon sticks to pan. Roast, basting hens occasionally with pan juices, until squash is tender and juices run clear when thickest part of thigh, next to body, is pierced with tip of knife, about 45 minutes longer.

6. To serve, cut each hen lengthwise in half (see Tip page 53). Arrange hens, squash, prunes, and cinnamon sticks on large platter. Skim and discard fat from drippings in pan; serve hens with pan juices.

Each serving: About 490 calories, 32g protein, 36g carbohydrate, 25g total fat (7g saturated), 176mg cholesterol, 360mg sodium.

Molasses-Glazed Cornish Hens

During the sugar refining process, the juice extracted from the sugar is boiled until syrupy—the result is molasses. Light (mild) molasses has the lightest flavor and color.

PREP: 5 MINUTES PLUS MARINATING   ROAST: 1 HOUR
MAKES 4 MAIN-DISH SERVINGS.

2 Cornish hens (1¹/₂ pounds each)   ¹/₄ teaspoon ground ginger
1 teaspoon ground allspice   ¹/₄ teaspoon salt
1 teaspoon dried thyme   2 tablespoons light (mild) molasses
¹/₂ teaspoon ground red pepper
  (cayenne)

1. Remove giblets and necks from hens; reserve for another use. Rinse hens inside and out with cold running water; drain. Pat hens dry with paper towels.

2. In large bowl, combine allspice, thyme, ground red pepper, ginger, and salt. Add hens, turning to coat. Cover and refrigerate the hens 2 hours to marinate.

3. Preheat oven to 375°F. With hens breast side up, lift wings up toward neck, then fold wing tips under back of hens so they stay in place. Tie legs together with string.

4. Place hens, breast side up, on rack in small roasting pan (13" by 9") and roast 40 minutes. Brush with molasses and roast, basting twice, until hens are tender and juices run clear when thickest part of thigh, next to body, is pierced with tip of knife, about 20 minutes longer. To serve, cut each hen lengthwise in half (see Tip page 53).

Each serving: About 402 calories, 32g protein, 8g carbohydrate, 26g total fat (7g saturated), 187mg cholesterol, 239mg sodium.

Cornish Hens with Wild Rice & Mushroom Stuffing

With the tasty mushroom and wild rice mixture stuffed under the skin, these crispy little birds make a great company dinner. Serve with steamed or creamed spinach.

PREP: 1 HOUR   ROAST: 50 MINUTES   MAKES 8 MAIN-DISH SERVINGS.

**Wild Rice & Mushroom Stuffing
  (page 59)**
4 Cornish hens (1^1/$_2$ pounds each)
^{1}/$_4$ cup honey

2 tablespoons fresh lemon juice
2 tablespoons dry vermouth
^{1}/$_2$ teaspoon salt
^{1}/$_4$ teaspoon dried thyme

1. Prepare Wild Rice & Mushroom Stuffing; set aside.

2. Preheat oven to 400°F. Remove giblets and necks from hens; reserve for another use. With poultry shears, cut each hen lengthwise in half (see Tip page 53). Rinse hen halves with cold running water; drain. Pat dry with paper towels.

3. With fingertips, carefully separate skin from meat on each hen half to form pocket; spoon some stuffing into each pocket. Place hens, skin side up, in 2 large roasting pans (17" by 11^1/$_2$").

4. In small bowl, combine honey, lemon juice, vermouth, salt, and thyme. Brush hens with some honey mixture. Roast hens, basting occasionally with remaining honey mixture and drippings in pan, until juices run clear when thickest part of thigh, next to body, is pierced with tip of knife, about 50 minutes, rotating pans between upper and lower oven racks halfway through the roasting.

5. To serve, arrange hens on dinner plates. Skim and disgard fat from drippings; serve hens with pan juices.

Wild Rice & Mushroom Stuffing

In 3-quart saucepan melt **1 tablespoon butter or margarine** over medium heat; add **1 small onion**, finely chopped, and cook until tender, about 5 minutes. Add **1 pound mushrooms**, trimmed and chopped, and cook, stirring occasionally, until tender, about 10 minutes. Meanwhile, rinse **1 cup (6 ounces) wild rice**; drain. To mixture in saucepan, add wild rice, **1 can (14 1/2 ounces) chicken broth**, and **1/4 teaspoon salt**; heat to boiling over high heat. Reduce heat; cover and simmer until the rice is tender and all liquid has been absorbed, 45 to 50 minutes. Stir in **1/4 cup chopped fresh parsley**. Makes 4 cups stuffing.

Each serving: About 521 calories, 37g protein, 30g carbohydrate, 28g total fat (8g saturated), 191mg cholesterol, 554mg sodium.

Cornish Hens Provençal

Made with tomatoes, garlic, and kalamata olives, this is the kind of robust dish for which the South of France is justly famous.

PREP: 10 MINUTES   ROAST: 50 MINUTES   MAKES 6 MAIN-DISH SERVINGS.

1 tablespoon olive oil
1 small garlic clove, minced
1/2 teaspoon dried thyme
1/2 teaspoon salt
1/4 teaspoon coarsely ground
  black pepper
3 Cornish hens (about
  1 1/4 pounds each)

2 large onions (12 ounces each),
  each cut into quarters
10 pitted Kalamata olives, coarsely
  chopped
3 large tomatoes, each cut into
  quarters

1. Preheat oven to 425°F. In cup, mix oil, garlic, thyme, salt, and pepper.
2. Remove giblets and necks from hens; reserve for another use. Rinse hens inside and out with cold running water; drain. Pat the hens dry with paper towels.
3. Lift wings up toward neck, then fold wing tips under back of hens so they stay in place. Tie legs of each hen together with string. Place hens, breast side up, in center of large roasting pan (17" by 11 1/2"). Rub with the oil mixture.
4. Arrange onions and olives around hens and roast, uncovered, 35 minutes, brushing hens occasionally with pan drippings. Add tomatoes and roast until juices run clear when thickest part of thigh, next to body, is pierced with tip of knife, 10 to 15 minutes longer.
5. Cut each hen lengthwise in half (see Tip page 53). Transfer hens and vegetables to a platter and keep warm. Skim and discard fat from pan juices; serve hens with pan juices.

Each serving: About 445 calories, 31g protein, 13g carbohydrate, 29g total fat (7g saturated), 174mg cholesterol, 460mg sodium.

Cornish Hen with Wild-Rice Pilaf

The colorful pilaf, made with carrot and sweet yellow pepper, simmers on the stovetop while the hens roast in the oven.

PREP: 60 TO 65 MINUTES   ROAST: 45 TO 50 MINUTES
MAKES 2 MAIN-DISH SERVINGS.

1 tablespoon olive oil	1 garlic clove, minced
1 large carrot, peeled and chopped	1 teaspoon chopped fresh oregano or
1 medium yellow pepper, chopped	1/4 teaspoon dried oregano
1 medium onion, chopped	1/4 teaspoon ground black pepper
1/2 cup wild rice, rinsed and drained	1 Cornish hen (11/4 pounds),
1/2 teaspoon salt	cut lengthwise in half (see Tip
1 cup water	page 53)

1. Prepare pilaf: In 2-quart saucepan, heat oil over medium-high heat. Add carrot, yellow pepper, and onion and cook, stirring frequently, until tender and lightly browned.

2. Stir in wild rice, 1/4 teaspoon salt, and water; heat to boiling over high heat. Reduce heat to low; cover and simmer until wild rice is tender and liquid has been absorbed, 45 to 50 minutes. Keep warm.

3. Meanwhile, preheat oven to 425°F. In small bowl, mix garlic, oregano, remaining 1/4 teaspoon salt, and pepper; rub mixture on hen halves. Place hen halves, skin side up, in small roasting pan (13" by 9").

4. Roast, brushing occasionally with pan drippings, until hen halves are browned and juices run clear when thickest part of hen is pierced with tip of knife, 45 to 50 minutes. Transfer hen halves to 2 warm dinner plates; keep warm.

5. With large spoon, skim and discard fat from the drippings in pan. Add *3 tablespoons hot water* to pan, stirring until browned bits are loosened from bottom of pan. Spoon pan juices over hen halves; serve with the Wild-Rice Pilaf.

Each serving: About 670 calories, 43g protein, 45g carbohydrate, 36g total fat (9g saturated), 203mg cholesterol, 655mg sodium.

TURKEY, GOOSE & DUCK

Roast Turkey with Wild-Mushroom Gravy

Classic Roast Turkey

We don't stuff our turkeys anymore, because we feel that cooking the stuffing separately yields a juicier bird. If you want to stuff your turkey, make sure the stuffing temperature reaches 165°. on a meat thermometer to be safe. Also, you will need to roast the turkey about 30 minutes longer than called for.

PREP: 45 MINUTES   ROAST: ABOUT 3 HOURS 45 MINUTES
MAKES 14 MAIN-DISH SERVINGS.

1 fresh or frozen (thawed; see Tip page 66) turkey (14 pounds)	1 1/2 teaspoons salt
1 large stalk celery, cut into pieces	1/2 teaspoon coarsely ground black pepper
1 medium onion, cut into quarters	1/2 teaspoon dried thyme
2 sprigs parsley	Giblet Gravy (page 66)

1. Preheat oven to 325°F. Remove giblets and neck from turkey; reserve for making Giblet Gravy. Rinse turkey inside and out with cold running water; drain well. Pat dry with paper towels.

2. Fasten neck skin to turkey back with one or two skewers. With turkey breast side up, lift wings up toward neck, then fold wing tips under back of turkey so they stay in place.

3. Place celery, onion, and parsley in body cavity. Close by folding skin over cavity opening; skewer closed if necessary. Tie legs and tail together with string, or push drumsticks under band of skin, or use stuffing clamp.

4. Place turkey, breast side up, on rack in large roasting pan (17" by 11 1/2"). Rub turkey all over with salt, pepper, and thyme. Cover turkey with loose tent of foil.

5. Roast turkey about 3 hours 45 minutes. Start checking for doneness during last hour of roasting.

6. While turkey is roasting, prepare the giblets and the neck to use in Giblet Gravy.

7. To brown turkey, remove foil during last hour of roasting time and occasionally baste with pan drippings. Turkey is done when temperature on meat thermometer inserted in thickest part of thigh, next to body, reaches 175° to 180°F and juices run clear when thickest part of thigh is pierced with tip of knife. (Breast temperature should be 165° to 170°F.)

8. Transfer turkey to large platter; keep warm. Let stand at least 15 minutes to set juices for easier carving.

9. Meanwhile, prepare Giblet Gravy.

10. Serve turkey with gravy. Remove skin from turkey before eating, if you like.

Each serving of turkey without skin or gravy: About 330 calories, 57g protein, 0g carbohydrate, 10g total fat (3g saturated), 150mg cholesterol, 330mg sodium.

Classic Roast Turkey

Giblet Gravy

In 3-quart saucepan, heat **gizzard**, **heart**, **neck**, and **4 cups water** to boiling over high heat. (Do not add liver; broth may taste bitter.) Reduce heat to low; cover and simmer 1 hour. Strain broth through sieve into large bowl, reserving meat and broth. Pull meat from neck; discard bones. Coarsely chop neck meat and giblets. Cover and refrigerate meat and giblet broth separately.

To make gravy, remove rack from roasting pan. Strain pan drippings through sieve into 4-cup liquid measuring cup or medium bowl. Add **1 cup giblet broth** to hot roasting pan and heat to boiling, stirring until browned bits are loosened from bottom of pan; add to drippings in measuring cup. Let stand until fat separates from pan juice, about 1 minute. Spoon **2 tablespoons fat** from pan juices into 2-quart saucepan; skim and discard any remaining fat from pan juices. Add **remaining giblet broth** and enough water to pan juices in cup to equal 3 cups.

Add **1/4 cup all-purpose flour** and **1/2 teaspoon salt** to fat in saucepan and cook over medium heat, stirring, until flour turns golden brown. Gradually stir in pan-juice mixture and cook, whisking, until gravy thickens slightly and boils; boil 1 minute. Stir in reserved giblets and neck meat; heat through. Pour into gravy boat. Makes about 3½ cups.

Each 1/4 cup gravy: About 70 calories, 7g protein, 2g carbohydrate, 3g total fat (1g saturated), 63mg cholesterol, 140mg sodium.

TIP

If using a frozen turkey, make sure it is completely thawed, especially inside the cavity. The rule of thumb for thawing turkey in the refrigerator is 24 hours per 5 pounds.

Herb-Scented Roast Turkey

Placing herbs and vegetables inside the turkey infuses the meat with flavor. To top it off—a luscious Roast Garlic-Balsamic Gravy.

PREP: 30 MINUTES   ROAST: 3 HOURS 45 MINUTES
MAKES 14 MAIN-DISH SERVINGS.

1 fresh or frozen (thawed; see Tip page 66) turkey (14 pounds)
1 medium onion, cut into 1-inch chunks
2 stalks celery, cut into 1-inch chunks
1/2 bunch fresh parsley
1 bunch fresh rosemary
1 bunch fresh sage
1 bunch fresh thyme
1 teaspoon salt
1 teaspoon coarsely ground black pepper
Roast Garlic-Balsamic Gravy (page 69)

1. Preheat oven to 325°F. Remove giblets and neck from turkey; reserve for gravy. Discard liver. Rinse turkey inside and out with cold running water; drain. Pat dry with paper towels.

2. Place onion, celery, parsley, and 1/2 bunch each of rosemary, sage, and thyme inside body and neck cavities of turkey. (Reserve remaining herbs for garnish, if you like.) Fasten neck skin to back with one or two skewers. With turkey breast side up, lift wings up toward neck, then fold wing tips under back of turkey so they stay in place. Tie legs together with string, or push drumsticks under band of skin, or use stuffing clamp.

3. Place turkey, breast side up, on small rack in large roasting pan (17" by 11 1/2"). Rub turkey all over with salt and pepper. Cut neck into several large pieces; scatter giblets and neck pieces around turkey in pan. Cover turkey with loose tent of foil.

4. Roast turkey about 3 hours 45 minutes; start checking for doneness during last hour of roasting.

5. To brown turkey, remove foil during last 1 hour 15 minutes of roasting time and occasionally baste with pan drippings. Turkey is done when temperature on meat thermometer inserted in thickest part of thigh, next to body, reaches 175° to 180°F and juices run clear when thigh is pierced with tip of knife. (Breast temperature should be 165°F to 170°F.)

6. Transfer turkey to large platter; keep warm. Let stand at least 15 minutes for easier carving.

Carving a Roast Turkey

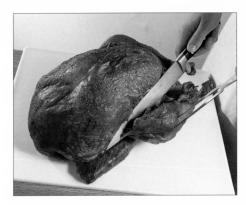

Cut through turkey skin where the leg is attached. To remove the leg, force it away from the body with a carving fork until it pops out of the socket. Separate the thigh from the body by cutting through the joint. If you like, separate the drumstick from the thigh by cutting through the center joint. To carve the leg, slice the thigh and drumstick meat, cutting parallel to the bones. Repeat on the other side.

To carve the breast, make a horizontal cut above the wing joint along the length of the bird, making sure to cut down to the bone.

With the knife parallel to the rib cage, cut the breast meat into thin slices. Cut off the wing. Repeat on the other side.

7. Prepare Roast Garlic–Balsamic Gravy.

8. Garnish platter with remaining rosemary, sage, and thyme sprigs, if you like. Serve turkey with gravy. Remove skin from turkey before eating, if you like.

Each serving turkey without skin or gravy: About 275 calories, 55g protein, 0g carbohydrate, 5g total fat (2g saturated), 180mg cholesterol, 290mg sodium.

Roast Garlic-Balsamic Gravy

While turkey is roasting, prepare roasted garlic: Remove any loose papery skin from **2 large whole heads garlic (8 ounces)**, leaving heads intact. Place garlic on sheet of heavy-duty foil; drizzle with **oil**. Wrap foil loosely around garlic and roast in 325°F oven with turkey until garlic is very soft, about 1 hour and 45 minutes. Set aside garlic until cool enough to handle, then separate garlic into cloves. Squeeze garlic from each clove into small bowl; set aside.

When turkey is done, pour drippings from roasting pan into 1-cup liquid measuring cup, leaving giblets and neck in pan. Let stand until fat separates from pan juices.

Meanwhile, spoon **3 tablespoons fat** from drippings into roasting pan. Discard any remaining fat. With wire whisk, stir **1/4 cup all-purpose flour** into fat in roasting pan; cook over medium heat 1 minute or until mixture turns golden brown, stirring constantly. Carefully add **1/3 cup balsamic vinegar** to hot roasting pan, stirring until browned bits are loosened from bottom or pan, about 30 seconds. Whisk in **2 cans (14 to 14 1/2 ounces each) chicken broth (3 1/2 cups), 6 sprigs fresh thyme, 1/4 teaspoon salt, 1/4 teaspoon coarsely ground black pepper**, roasted garlic, **reserved pan juices**, and **2/3 cup water**; heat to boiling over medium-high heat. Boil, stirring frequently, 5 minutes. Discard neck and giblets.

Strain gravy through medium-mesh sieve into medium bowl, pressing garlic with rubber spatula or back of spoon through sieve; stir until well combined. Transfer gravy to gravy boat.

Each 1/4 cup: About 65 calories, 2g protein, 7g carbohydrate, 4g total fat (1g saturated), 3mg cholesterol, 265mg sodium.

Apple-Glazed Turkey with Multigrain-Bread Stuffing

The cinnamon-and-clove-scented glaze smells wonderful cooking and tastes great too. For a more nutritious stuffing, we tried multigrain bread with delicious results.

PREP: 30 MINUTES PLUS MAKING GRAVY
ROAST: ABOUT 3 HOURS 45 MINUTES
MAKES 14 MAIN-DISH SERVINGS.

3 tablespoons butter or margarine
7 medium stalks celery, chopped
3 medium onions, chopped
1 cup water
3/4 teaspoon dried oregano
1 1/2 loaves (24 ounces total) multigrain bread, cut into 1/2-inch cubes

1 can (14 1/2 ounces) chicken broth
1 1/4 teaspoons coarsely ground black pepper
1 ready-to-stuff turkey (14 pounds), giblets and neck reserved for Giblet Gravy (page 66)
1 1/2 teaspoons salt
Apple Glaze (page 71)

1. Prepare stuffing: In 12-inch skillet, melt butter over medium heat; add celery and onions and cook, stirring frequently, until golden. Stir in 1/4 cup water. Reduce the heat to low; cover and cook until the vegetables are tender.

2. Transfer cooked vegetables to very large bowl. Add oregano, bread, broth, 3/4 teaspoon pepper, and remaining 3/4 cup water. Set aside.

3. Preheat oven to 325°F. Remove giblets and neck from turkey; reserve for making Giblet Gravy (see page 66). Rinse turkey inside and out with cold running water; drain well. Pat dry with paper towels.

4. Loosely spoon some stuffing into neck cavity. Fold neck skin over stuffing; fasten neck skin to back with one or two skewers. Loosely spoon remaining stuffing into body cavity. Fold skin over cavity opening; skewer closed, if necessary. (Place any leftover stuffing in greased, covered casserole and add to oven 30 minutes before end of roasting time.) Tie legs and tail together with string, or push drumsticks under band of skin, or use stuffing clamp. Secure wings to body with string, if desired.

5. Place turkey, breast side up, on rack in large roasting pan (17" by 11½"). Sprinkle salt and remaining ½ teaspoon pepper on outside of turkey. Cover turkey with loose tent of foil.

6. Roast turkey about 3 hours 45 minutes. Start checking for doneness during last hour of roasting (see below).

7. To brown turkey, remove foil during last hour of roasting and baste occasionally with pan drippings. Turkey is done when temperature on meat thermometer inserted in thickest part of thigh, next to body, reaches 175° to 180°F and juices run clear when thickest part of thigh is pierced with tip of knife. (Breast temperature should be 165° to 170°F; stuffing temperature should be 165°F).

8. Meanwhile, prepare broth for Giblet Gravy, page 66.

9. Prepare Apple Glaze. About 10 minutes before end of roasting time, brush turkey with glaze.

10. Transfer turkey to large warm platter; keep warm. Let stand at least 15 minutes for easier carving. Prepare Giblet Gravy (page 66) and serve with turkey.

About 630 calories, 61g protein, 36g carbohydrate, 25g total fat (8g saturated), 222mg cholesterol, 847mg sodium

---

TIP

Turkey is done when temperature on meat thermometer inserted in thickest part of thigh reaches 175°F to 180°F and juices run clear when thickest part of thigh is pierced with tip of knife. (Breast temperature should be 165° to 170°F; stuffing temperature should be 165°F.)

Apple Glaze

In 1-quart saucepan, heat **½ cup apple jelly**, **3 tablespoons balsamic vinegar**, **½ teaspoon ground cinnamon**, and **¼ teaspoon ground cloves** to boiling over medium-high heat. Boil, stirring constantly, until mixture thickens slightly, about 2 minutes.

Roast Turkey with Wild-Mushroom Gravy

White, shiitake, and dried porcini mushrooms add rich flavor to classic giblet gravy.

PREP: 1 HOUR   ROAST: ABOUT 3 HOURS 45 MINUTES
MAKES 14 MAIN-DISH SERVINGS.

TURKEY
1 fresh or frozen (thawed; see Tip page 66) turkey (14 pounds)
1 1/2 teaspoons salt
1/2 teaspoon coarsely ground black pepper

WILD-MUSHROOM GRAVY
giblets and neck from turkey
4 cups cold water

1 package (1/3 ounce) dried porcini mushrooms (about 1/3 cup)
1 cup boiling water
1 tablespoon butter or margarine
1 medium shallot, minced (1/4 cup)
10 ounces white mushrooms, trimmed and sliced
8 ounces shiitake mushrooms, stems removed and caps thinly sliced
1/4 cup all-purpose flour
1/4 teaspoon salt

1. Preheat oven to 325°F. Remove giblets and neck from turkey; reserve for making gravy. Rinse turkey inside and out; drain well. Pat dry with paper towels.

2. Fasten neck skin to turkey back with one or two skewers. With turkey breast side up, lift wings up toward neck and fold wing tips under back of turkey so they stay in place. Tie legs and tail together with string, or push drumsticks under band of skin, or use stuffing clamp.

3. Place turkey, breast side up, on roasting rack in large roasting pan (17" by 11 1/2"). Sprinkle outside of turkey with salt and pepper. Cover turkey with loose tent of foil.

4. Roast turkey about 3 hours 45 minutes. Start checking for doneness during last hour of roasting (see Tip page 71).

5. While turkey is roasting, begin Wild-Mushroom Gravy: In 3-quart saucepan, combine turkey gizzard, heart, neck, and cold water; heat to boiling over high heat. Reduce heat to low; cover and simmer 45 minutes. Strain giblet broth through sieve into large bowl; reserve broth; Discard giblets and neck. Cover and refrigerate broth.

Roast Turkey with Wild-Mushroom Gravy

6. Meanwhile, in small bowl, soak dried porcini mushrooms in the boiling water 30 minutes. With slotted spoon, remove porcini from soaking liquid, reserving liquid. Rinse porcini to remove grit; slice. Strain soaking liquid through sieve lined with paper towel in small bowl or cup; set aside.

7. In nonstick 12-inch skillet, melt butter over medium-low heat. Add shallot and cook until tender, stirring occasionally, about 10 minutes. Increase heat to medium-high; add white, shiitake, and porcini mushrooms and cook, stirring occasionally, until tender and golden, about 15 minutes. Add porcini soaking liquid; heat to boiling and cook 1 minute. Transfer mixture to medium bowl.

8. To brown turkey, remove foil during last hour of roasting time and baste occasionally with pan drippings. Turkey is done when temperature on meat thermometer inserted into thickest part of thigh, next to body, reaches 175° to 180°F and juices run clear when thickest part of thigh is pierced with knife. (Breast temperature should reach 165° to 170°F.)

9. Transfer turkey to large platter; keep warm.

10. Prepare Wild-Mushroom Gravy: Remove rack from roasting pan. Strain pan drippings through sieve into 8-cup glass measuring cup or medium bowl. Add 1 cup giblet broth to hot roasting pan and heat to boiling, stirring until browned bits are loosened from bottom of pan; strain through sieve into measuring cup. Let stand until fat separates from pan juices, about 1 minute. Spoon 2 tablespoons fat from drippings into 3-quart saucepan; skim and discard any remaining fat. Add mushroom mixture and enough of the broth (about 2 cups) to pan juices in cup to equal 5 cups.

11. Add flour and salt into fat in saucepan and cook over medium heat, stirring, until flour turns goldenbrown. Gradually stir in mushroom mixture and cook, stirring, until gravy boils and thickens slightly. Pour gravy into gravy boat. Makes about 6 cups gravy.

12. Serve turkey with gravy. Remove skin before eating, if you like.

Each serving of turkey without skin or gravy: About 330 calories, 57g protein, 0g carbohydrate, 10g total fat (3g saturated), 149mg cholesterol, 330mg sodium.

Each 1/4 cup gravy: About 30 calories, 1g protein, 3g carbohydrate, 2g total fat (1g saturated), 3mg cholesterol, 62mg sodium.

Turkey with Port Wine Sauce & Rice Stuffing

Try this for a wonderful combination of flavors: rice stuffing studded with currants, paired with our cranberry-raspberry glazed turkey and Port Wine Sauce. Yum.

PREP: 35 MINUTES   ROAST: 3 HOURS
MAKES 6 MAIN-DISH SERVINGS.

1¹/₂ cups aromatic rice (such as
   Texmati or jasmine) or regular
   long-grain rice
1³/₄ teaspoons salt
3 medium stalks celery
1 medium onion
2 tablespoons vegetable oil
¹/₃ cup dried currants
1 ready-to-stuff turkey or capon
   (8 pounds)

¹/₂ teaspoon dried thyme
2 cups cranberry-raspberry juice
2 tablespoons brown sugar
¹/₄ cup cranberries, sliced
2 tablespoons Port wine
2 teaspoons cornstarch
¹/₂ teaspoon chicken-flavor instant
   bouillon

1. Prepare stuffing: In 3-quart saucepan, prepare rice as label directs, using ³/₄ teaspoon salt. Meanwhile, thinly slice celery; finely chop onion. In 10-inch skillet, heat oil over medium heat; add celery and onion and cook until vegetables are lightly browned. Stir in ¹/₂ cup water; heat to boiling over high heat. Reduce heat to low; simmer, uncovered, until water has evaporated and vegetables are tender. Add vegetable mixture and currants to cooked rice; toss to combine. Set stuffing aside.

2. Preheat oven to 350°F. Remove giblets and neck from turkey; reserve for another use. Rinse turkey inside and out with cold running water; drain well. Pat dry with paper towels.

3. Loosely spoon some stuffing into neck cavity. Fold neck skin over stuffing; fasten neck skin to back with one or two skewers. Loosely spoon remaining stuffing into body cavity. Fold skin over cavity opening; skewer closed, if necessary. (Place any leftover stuffing in greased, covered casserole and add to oven 30 minutes before end of roasting time.) Tie legs and tail together with string, or push drumsticks under band of skin, or use stuffing clamp. Secure wings to body with string, if desired.

4. Place turkey, breast side up, on rack in large roasting pan (17" by 11½"). Rub thyme and remaining 1 teaspoon salt on outside of turkey. Cover with loose tent of foil. Roast about 3 hours. Turkey is done when temperature on meat thermometer inserted into thickest part of thigh, next to body, reaches 175° to 180°F and juices run clear when thickest part of thigh is pierced with knife. (Breast temperature should reach 165° to 170°F.)

5. Prepare glaze: In 3-quart saucepan, heat cranberry-raspberry juice and brown sugar to boiling over high heat. Cook, uncovered, until mixture has reduced to ⅓ cup, about 15 minutes. Cover and set aside.

6. Transfer turkey to warm platter; keep warm. Let stand 15 minutes to set juices for easier carving. Reserve pan drippings.

7. Prepare sauce: Remove rack from roasting pan; skim and discard fat from drippings in pan. Add *½ cup water* to pan; stirring until browned bits are loosened from bottom of pan. Strain mixture through sieve into 1-quart saucepan. Add cranberries and ¼ cup glaze. Heat to boiling over high heat; boil until mixture thickens, about 1 minute. In cup, mix port, cornstarch, bouillon, and *⅓ cup water*. Stir into sauce; heat to boiling. Boil 1 minute; pour into gravy boat.

8. Brush turkey with remaining glaze. Serve turkey with Port Wine Sauce and stuffing.

Each serving: About 825 calories, 72g protein, 65g carbohydrate, 28g total fat (8g saturated), 233mg cholesterol, 895mg sodium.

Turkey with Roasted Apples

No need for cranberry sauce when you have tender sweet roasted apples to accompany your turkey. Serve it with a simple pan gravy, or add a dash of Port wine if you prefer.

Prep: 45 minutes   Roast: 3 hours 45 minutes
Makes 14 main-dish servings.

1 fresh or frozen (thawed; see Tip page 66) turkey (14 pounds)
1 1/2 teaspoons salt
1/2 teaspoon coarsely ground black pepper
6 medium Gala apples

EASY PAN GRAVY OR PORT WINE GRAVY
giblets and neck from turkey
1 medium onion, cut in half

1 stalk celery, cut into 3-inch pieces
1 bay leaf
4 cups water
1/4 cup all-purpose flour
1/2 teaspoon salt
3/4 cup tawny Port wine (for Port Wine Gravy)

1. Preheat oven to 325°F. Remove giblets and neck from turkey; reserve for making gravy. Rinse turkey inside and out with cold running water; drain well. Pat dry with paper towels.

2. Fasten neck skin to turkey back with one or two skewers. With turkey breast side up, lift wings up toward neck, then fold wing tips under back of turkey so they stay in place. Tie legs and tail together with string, or push drumsticks under band of skin, or use stuffing clamp.

3. Place turkey, breast side up, on small rack in large roasting pan (17" by 11 1/2"). Rub turkey all over with salt and pepper. Cover turkey with a loose tent of foil. Roast turkey about 3 hours 45 minutes. Start checking for doneness during last hour of roasting.

4. While turkey is roasting, prepare giblet broth for either Easy Pan Gravy or Port Wine Gravy. In 3-quart saucepan, heat giblets, neck (do not add liver), onion, celery, bay leaf, and water to boiling over high heat. Reduce heat to low; cover and simmer 45 minutes. Strain broth through sieve into large bowl, reserving meat and broth. Pull meat from neck; discard bones. Coarsely chop neck meat and the giblets.

5. About 1 hour 15 minutes before turkey is done, cut each apple lengthwise in half. Remove foil from turkey. Add apples to roasting pan around

Turkey with Roasted Apples

turkey; brush generously with pan drippings. Roast turkey and the apples, basting turkey occasionally with pan drippings, 1 hour, turning apples over once halfway through roasting.

6. Turkey is done when temperature on meat thermometer inserted in thickest part of thigh, next to body, reaches 175° to 180°F and breast temperature reaches 165°F. Internal temperature will rise 5° to 10°F upon standing.

7. When turkey is done, transfer turkey and apples to large platter; cover with foil to keep warm.

8. Remove rack from roasting pan. Strain pan drippings through sieve into 4-cup liquid measuring cup or medium bowl. Add 1 cup giblet broth to roasting pan (if making Port Wine Gravy, substitute 3/4 cup tawny Port wine for 1 cup giblet broth); heat to boiling over medium-high heat, stirring until browned bits are loosened from bottom of pan. Boil 1 minute. Strain liquid into drippings in measuring cup. Let stand until fat separates from pan juices, about 1 minute. Spoon 2 tablespoons fat from drippings into 2-quart saucepan; skim and discard any remaining fat from pan juices. Add remaining giblet broth and enough *water* to pan juices in cup to equal 3 cups total. (If you have any leftover giblet broth, save for another use.)

9. Add flour and salt to fat in saucepan and cook over medium heat, stirring, until flour turns golden brown. Gradually stir in pan-juice mixture and cook, stirring, until gravy boils and thickens slightly. For Easy Pan Gravy, stir in reserved giblets and neck meat; heat through. Pour gravy into gravy boat. Makes about 3 1/2 cups.

10. Serve turkey with apples and gravy.

Each serving turkey without skin, apples, or gravy: About 245 calories, 48g protein, 0g carbohydrate, 4g total fat (1g saturated), 160mg cholesterol, 235mg sodium.

Each 1/4 cup Easy Pan Gravy: About 55 calories, 5g protein, 2g carbohydrate, 3g total fat (1g saturated), 63mg cholesterol, 130mg sodium.

Each 1/4 cup Port Wine Gravy: About 45 calories, 7g protein, 1g carbohydrate, 3g total fat (1g saturated), 3mg cholesterol, 130mg sodium.

Roast Turkey Breast with Caramelized Shallots

Richly caramelized shallots add color, flavor, and moistness to roasted turkey breast.

PREP: 40 MINUTES   ROAST: 2 HOURS 30 MINUTES TO 3 HOURS
MAKES 10 MAIN-DISH SERVINGS.

1 tablespoon olive oil
8 ounces shallots or red onion, thinly
  sliced (2 cups)
4 garlic cloves, thinly sliced
2 tablespoons brown sugar
2 tablespoons plus 1/2 cup water
1 tablespoon balsamic vinegar
1/2 teaspoon salt

1/4 teaspoon coarsely ground
  black pepper
1 bone-in turkey breast (6 to
  7 pounds)
1/2 cup dry red wine
1 cup chicken broth
1 tablespoon cornstarch

1. In nonstick 10-inch skillet, heat oil over medium-high heat. Add shallots and cook, stirring occasionally, until tender and deep golden, about 8 to 10 minutes. Add garlic and cook 1 minute longer. Stir in brown sugar, 1 tablespoon water, vinegar, salt, and pepper; cook 1 minute. Transfer to small bowl and cool to room temperature.

2. Preheat oven to 325°F. Rinse turkey breast with cold running water and drain well; pat dry with paper towels. With fingertips, gently separate skin from meat on turkey breast. Spread cooled shallot mixture on meat under skin.

3. Place turkey, skin side up, on rack in medium roasting pan (14" by 10"). Cover turkey with loose tent of foil.

4. Roast turkey 1 hour 30 minutes. Remove foil; roast 1 to 1 hour 30 minutes longer, occasionally basting with pan drippings. Turkey breast is done when temperature on meat thermometer inserted in thickest part of breast (not touching bone) reaches 165°F and juices run clear when thickest part of breast is pierced with tip of knife. Internal temperature of meat will rise to 170°F upon standing.

5. Transfer turkey to warm platter. Let stand 15 minutes to set juices for easier carving.

6. Meanwhile, prepare sauce: Remove rack from roasting pan. Skim and discard fat from drippings in pan. In 2-quart saucepan, heat wine to boiling over medium heat; boil 2 minutes. Stir in broth, 1/2 cup water, and pan juices; heat to boiling. In cup, blend cornstarch with remaining 1 tablespoon water until smooth. With wire whisk, whisk into sauce and boil, stirring, 1 minute. Strain through sieve into gravy boat. Serve with turkey.

Each serving with skin and sauce: About 400 calories, 53g protein, 8g carbohydrate, 15g total fat (4g saturated), 136mg cholesterol, 336mg sodium.

Turkey Breast with Mushroom Filling

Roast a delicious sauté of finely chopped mushrooms, onion, and garlic under the turkey skin for a flavorful twist. To save time and stress on the big day, make the mushroom mixture two days ahead.

PREP: 45 MINUTES   ROAST: 2 HOURS 30 MINUTES TO 3 HOURS
MAKES 10 MAIN-DISH SERVINGS.

MUSHROOM FILLING

- 2 packages (10 ounces each) mushrooms
- 1 medium onion, cut into quarters
- 2 garlic cloves, peeled
- 2 tablespoons butter or margarine
- 1/2 teaspoon salt
- 1/4 teaspoon coarsely ground black pepper

TURKEY AND GRAVY

- 1 bone-in turkey breast (7 pounds)
- 1/2 teaspoon salt
- 1/4 teaspoon coarsely ground black pepper
- 2 tablespoons cornstarch
- 1/2 cup water
- 1/2 cup dry red wine
- 1 can (14 1/2 ounces) chicken broth

1. Prepare filling: In food processor with knife blade attached, pulse mushrooms, onion, and garlic, one-third at a time, until finely chopped.

2. In nonstick 12-inch skillet, heat butter over medium-high heat until melted. Add mushroom mixture, salt, and pepper and cook, stirring frequently, until mixture is dry and golden, about 25 minutes. Transfer mushroom mixture to plate; cover with foil or plastic wrap and refrigerate mixture until cool.

3. Preheat oven to 325°F. With fingertips, gently separate skin from meat on turkey breast. Spread cooked mushroom mixture on meat under skin. Sprinkle salt and pepper on outside of turkey.

4. Place turkey breast, skin side up, on rack in medium roasting pan (14" by 10"). Cover turkey breast with loose tent of foil.

5. Roast turkey 2 hours 30 minutes to 3 hours. Start checking for doneness during last 30 minutes of roasting. Turkey breast is done when temperature on meat thermometer inserted in thickest part of breast, not touching bone, reaches 165°F, and juices run clear when thickest part of

Turkey Breast with Mushroom Filling

breast is pierced with tip of knife. Internal temperature of meat will rise to 170°F upon standing.

6. To brown turkey breast, remove foil during last hour of roasting time. Transfer turkey to warm platter. Let stand 15 minutes to set the juices for easier slicing.

7. Meanwhile, prepare gravy: Remove rack from roasting pan. Skim and discard fat from drippings in pan. In cup, blend cornstarch with water until smooth; set aside. Add red wine to hot roasting pan; heat to boiling over medium-high heat, stirring until browned bits are loosened from bottom of pan. Boil 2 minutes. Pour mixture into 2-quart saucepan. Whisk in broth and cornstarch mixture; heat to boiling. Boil 1 minute. Strain through sieve into gravy boat. Serve turkey with gravy.

Each serving without gravy: About 425 calories, 60g protein, 4g carbohydrate, 18g total fat (6g saturated), 157mg cholesterol, 388mg sodium.

Each 1/4 cup gravy: About 15 calories, 1g protein, 2g carbohydrate, 0g total fat, 0mg cholesterol, 190mg sodium.

Rosemary Roast Turkey Breast

When a whole turkey is too much, just use the breast. It will make white meat fans very happy.

Prep: 20 minutes   Roast: 2 hours 15 minutes to 2 hours 30 minutes
Makes 10 main-dish servings.

1 bone-in turkey breast (6 to 7 pounds)
1½ teaspoons dried rosemary, crumbled
1 teaspoon salt
¾ teaspoon coarsely ground black pepper
1 cup chicken broth

1. Preheat oven to 350°F. Rinse turkey breast with cold running water; drain well. Pat dry with paper towels. In cup, combine rosemary, salt, and pepper. Rub rosemary mixture on inside and outside of turkey breast.

2. Place turkey, skin side up, on rack in small roasting pan (13" by 9"). Cover turkey with loose tent of foil.

3. Roast turkey 1 hour 30 minutes. Remove foil. Roast 45 to 60 minutes longer, occasionally basting with pan drippings. Start checking for doneness during last 30 minutes of cooking. Turkey breast is done when temperature on meat thermometer inserted in thickest part of breast (not touching bone) reaches 165°F and juices run clear when thickest part of breast is pierced with tip of knife. Internal temperature of meat will rise to 170°F upon standing.

4. Transfer turkey to warm platter. Let stand 15 minutes to set juices for easier carving.

5. Meanwhile, pour broth into drippings in hot roasting pan; heat to boiling, stirring until browned bits are loosened from bottom of pan. Strain pan-juice mixture through sieve into 1-quart saucepan. Let stand until fat has separated from pan-juice mixture, about 1 minute. Skim and discard fat. Heat pan-juice mixture over medium heat until hot; serve with turkey. Remove skin before eating.

Each serving without skin and with pan juices: About 251 calories, 55g protein, 0g carbohydrate, 2g total fat (0g saturated), 152mg cholesterol, 428mg sodium.

Turkey Breast with Roasted Vegetable Gravy

Although we slimmed down this Thanksgiving centerpiece by serving a turkey breast without its skin, degreasing the drippings, and thickening the gravy with roasted vegetables, your guests will never know it's healthier!

PREP: 40 MINUTES   ROAST: 2 HOURS
MAKES 8 MAIN-DISH SERVINGS.

1 bone-in turkey breast (6 pounds)	2 carrots, peeled and cut into 3-inch
1/2 teaspoon salt	pieces
1/4 teaspoon ground black pepper	3 garlic cloves, peeled
2 medium onions, each cut into	1/2 teaspoon dried thyme
quarters	1 can (14 1/2 ounces) chicken broth
2 stalks celery, cut into 3-inch pieces	1 cup water

1. Preheat oven to 350°F. Rinse turkey breast inside and out with cold running water and drain well. Pat dry with paper towels. Rub outside of turkey with salt and pepper.

2. Place the turkey breast, skin side up, on rack in medium roasting pan (14" by 10").

3. Scatter onions, celery, carrots, garlic, and thyme around turkey in roasting pan. Cover turkey with loose tent of foil. Roast turkey 1 hour. Remove foil and roast 1 hour to 1 hour and 15 minutes longer. Start checking for doneness during last 30 minutes of roasting. Turkey breast is done when temperature on meat thermometer inserted in thickest part of breast (not touching bone) reaches 165°F and juices run clear when thickest part of breast is pierced with tip of knife. Internal temperature of meat will rise to 170°F upon standing.

4. Transfer turkey to warm platter. Let stand 15 minutes to set juices for easier carving.

5. Meanwhile, prepare gravy: Remove rack from roasting pan. Pour vegetables and pan drippings into sieve set over 4-cup liquid measure or

Turkey Breast with Roasted Vegetable Gravy

medium bowl; transfer solids to blender. Let juices stand until fat separates from pan juices, about 1 minute. Skim and discard fat from drippings.

6. Add broth to hot roasting pan and heat to boiling, stirring until browned bits are loosened from bottom of pan. Pour broth mixture through sieve into pan juices in measuring cup.

7. In blender puree reserved solids with pan juices and water until smooth. Pour puree into 2-quart saucepan; heat to boiling over high heat. Makes about 4 cups gravy.

8. To serve, remove skin from turkey. Serve sliced turkey with gravy.

Each serving turkey without skin: About 285 calories, 63g protein, 0g carbohydrate, 2g total fat (1g saturated), 174mg cholesterol, 255mg sodium.

Each 1/4 cup gravy: About 20 calories, 1g protein, 3g carbohydrate, 0g total fat, 0mg cholesterol, 125mg sodium.

Rolled Turkey Breast with Basil Mayonnaise

Here's a dramatic-looking party entrée that takes very little effort.

PREP: 45 MINUTES   ROAST: 1 HOUR 15 MINUTES
MAKES 10 MAIN-DISH SERVINGS.

1 whole boneless turkey breast
(4¹/₂ to 5 pounds), cut in half
2 teaspoons salt
1 teaspoon coarsely ground
black pepper
1 jar (12 ounces) roasted red
peppers, drained

1¹/₂ cups loosely packed fresh basil
leaves plus additional sprigs
1 tablespoon olive oil
Basil Mayonnaise (page 91)

1. To butterfly breast halves, place 1 breast half, skinned side up, on cutting board. With sharp knife held parallel to surface, and starting at one long side, horizontally cut turkey breast half three-fourths of the way through and open like a book. With meat mallet, or between two sheets of plastic wrap or waxed paper with rolling pin, pound turkey breast half to about ¹/₄-inch thickness. Repeat with second breast half.

2. Preheat oven to 350°F. Sprinkle ¹/₂ teaspoon salt and ¹/₄ teaspoon black pepper on each breast half. Arrange roasted red peppers evenly over breast halves, leaving 2-inch border around edges; top with basil leaves. Starting at one narrow end, roll each breast half jelly-roll fashion. Tie each turkey roll with string at 2-inch intervals; brush with oil and sprinkle with remaining 1 teaspoon salt and remaining ¹/₂ teaspoon pepper.

3. Place turkey rolls, seam side down, on rack in large roasting pan (17" by 11¹/₂"). Roast turkey rolls about 1 hour 15 minutes. Turkey is done when temperature on meat thermometer inserted in center of roll reaches 160°F. Internal temperature of turkey will rise to 165°F upon standing.

4. Transfer rolls to warm platter; let stand 10 minutes to set juices for easier slicing if serving warm. If not serving right away, cool turkey 1 hour; wrap in plastic wrap and refrigerate up to 24 hours to serve cold later.

Rolled Turkey Breast with Basil Mayonnaise

5. To serve, remove strings. Cut turkey roll crosswise into thin slices, garnish with basil sprigs, and serve with Basil Mayonnaise.

Each serving without Basil Mayonnaise: About 268 calories, 53g protein, 5g carbohydrate, 3g total fat (1g saturated), 133mg cholesterol, 638mg sodium.

Basil Mayonnaise

In blender or in food processor with knife blade attached, puree **2 cups loosely packed fresh basil leaves**, **1 cup light mayonnaise**, **1 cup reduced-fat sour cream**, **2 teaspoons fresh lemon juice**, and **1/4 teaspoon salt** until smooth. Cover and refrigerate until ready to use. Makes 2 cups mayonnaise.

Each tablespoon: About 40 calories, 1g protein, 1g carbohydrate, 4g total fat (1g saturated), 5mg cholesterol, 80mg sodium.

Turkey Bacon Breast with Winter Vegetables

Crisp bacon, caramelized onions, and garlic are roasted under the turkey skin for extra flavor.

PREP: 40 MINUTES ROAST: 2 HOURS 30 MINUTES
MAKES 10 MAIN-DISH SERVINGS.

4 slices bacon, chopped
1 medium red onion, chopped
2 large garlic cloves, thinly sliced
1 teaspoon dried thyme
3/4 teaspoon salt
1/2 teaspoon coarsely ground
  black pepper
2 tablespoons plus 1/3 cup water
1 bone-in turkey breast
  (6 1/2 pounds)

2 pounds Yukon Gold potatoes,
  each cut into quarters
1 pound carrots, peeled and cut into
  2-inch pieces
1 large onion (12 ounces), cut into
  8 wedges
1 tablespoon vegetable oil
1/4 cup dry white wine
1 cup chicken broth
1 tablespoon cornstarch

1. In 10-inch skillet, cook bacon over medium heat until browned. With slotted spoon, transfer bacon to paper towels to drain. Discard all but 1 tablespoon bacon drippings from skillet; add chopped onion and cook, stirring frequently, until golden and tender, about 10 minutes. Add the garlic, 1/2 teaspoon thyme, 1/2 teaspoon salt, and 1/4 teaspoon pepper; cook, stirring, 3 minutes longer. Add 2 tablespoons water, stirring until browned bits are loosened from bottom of pan; cook 1 minute. Transfer onion mixture to small bowl; stir in bacon. Set aside until cool enough to handle.

2. Preheat oven to 325°F. With fingertips, gently separate skin from meat on turkey breast. Spread cooled onion mixture on meat under skin.

3. Place turkey breast, skin side up, on small rack in large roasting pan (17" by 11 1/2").

4. In large bowl, toss the potatoes, carrots, onion wedges, oil, remaining 1/2 teaspoon thyme, 1/4 teaspoon salt, and 1/4 teaspoon pepper. Arrange vegetables in roasting pan around turkey breast. Cover turkey breast (not vegetables) with loose tent of foil.

5. Roast turkey about 2 hours 30 minutes. Start checking for doneness during last 30 minutes of roasting. Turkey breast is done when temperature on meat thermometer inserted in thickest part of breast (not touching bone) reaches 165°F and juices run clear when thickest part of breast is pierced with tip of knife. Internal temperature of meat will rise to 170°F upon standing.

6. Transfer turkey to platter; keep warm. Let turkey stand 15 minutes to set juices for easier carving.

7. Meanwhile, transfer vegetables to bowl. Remove rack from roasting pan. Pour drippings into cup; let stand until fat separates from pan juices. Skim and discard fat from pan juices. Reserve pan juices. Turn oven control to 450°F.

8. Return vegetables to roasting pan and roast until brown and crisp, about 15 minutes. Transfer vegetables to serving platter; keep warm.

9. Prepare gravy: Pour wine into hot roasting pan; cook 2 minutes over medium heat, stirring until browned bits are loosened from bottom of the pan. Pour wine mixture into 1-quart saucepan; stir in broth and reserved pan juices. In cup, with small wire whisk or fork, blend cornstarch and $^{1}/_{3}$ cup water until smooth. Slowly whisk cornstarch mixture into wine mixture; heat over high heat, whisking constantly, until gravy boils and thickens slightly. Boil 1 minute.

10. Serve gravy with turkey and vegetables.

Each serving: About 355 calories, 39g protein, 23g carbohydrate, 11g total fat (3g saturated), 76mg cholesterol, 930mg sodium.

Turkey Pinwheels

A butterflied and flattened turkey breast is spread with a vegetable filling, rolled up, tied, and roasted. The dazzling presentation is worth the extra effort.

PREP: 45 MINUTES   ROAST: 1 HOUR 15 MINUTES TO 1 HOUR 30 MINUTES
MAKES 8 MAIN-DISH SERVINGS.

2 tablespoons plus 2 teaspoons
  vegetable oil
1 bag (16 ounces) carrots, diced
2 medium onions, diced
1 large red pepper, diced
1 medium stalk celery, diced
1 3/4 teaspoons salt
1/2 cup water
2 tablespoons plain dried
  bread crumbs

2 tablespoons freshly grated
  Parmesan cheese
1/4 cup chopped fresh parsley
1 skinless, boneless turkey breast
  half (2 1/2 pounds)
1 teaspoon coarsely ground
  black pepper

1. In 12-inch skillet, heat 2 tablespoons oil over medium-high heat. Add carrots, onions, red pepper, celery, and 1 teaspoon salt and cook, stirring frequently, until vegetables are well browned, about 15 minutes.

2. To vegetables in skillet, add water; heat to boiling over high heat. Reduce heat to low; cover and simmer until vegetables are tender, about 5 minutes. Remove cover; cook until any liquid in skillet has evaporated.

3. Remove skillet from heat. Stir in bread crumbs, Parmesan, and 2 table-spoons chopped parsley.

4. Preheat oven to 325°F. To butterfly breast half, place breast half, skin side down, on cutting board. With sharp knife held parallel to work surface, and starting at one long side, horizontally cut breast half three-fourths of the way through and open like a book. With meat mallet or rolling pin, pound turkey breast half between two sheets of plastic wrap or waxed paper into a 14" by 12" rectangle.

5. Spread vegetable mixture evenly over breast half. Starting from one long side, roll turkey, jelly-roll fashion, to enclose stuffing completely. Tie turkey roll securely with string at 1 1/2-inch intervals; place on rack in small roasting pan (13" by 9").

6. In cup, mix black pepper, remaining 3/4 teaspoon salt, 2 teaspoons oil, and remaining 2 tablespoons chopped parsley; pat mixture over turkey breast roll.

7. Roast, brushing occasionally with pan drippings, 1 hour 15 minutes to 1 hour 30 minutes. Turkey is done when thermometer inserted in center of roll reaches 160°F. Internal temperature of turkey will rise to 165°F upon standing. Transfer turkey roll to cutting board; keep warm. Let stand 15 minutes to set juices for easier slicing.

8. To serve, remove strings. Cut roll crosswise into 1/2-inch-thick slices. Transfer turkey slices to warm large platter.

Each serving: About 263 calories, 38g protein, 12g carbohydrate, 6g total fat (1g saturated), 90mg cholesterol, 608mg sodium.

Christmas Goose

What could be more traditional than a Christmas goose! This one, however, is a little different from the usual: It is flavored with sugar, soy sauce, and ginger.

PREP: 20 MINUTES ROAST: 3 HOURS TO 3 HOURS 30 MINUTES
MAKES 10 MAIN-DISH SERVINGS.

1 goose (14 pounds)
1 teaspoon salt
1/2 teaspoon ground black pepper
1/2 teaspoon ground sage
3 tablespoons sugar
3 tablespoons soy sauce
3 tablespoons red wine vinegar

1 tablespoon minced, peeled fresh
  ginger or 3/4 teaspoon
  ground ginger
3 tablespoons all-purpose flour
1 beef-flavor bouillon cube
  or envelope

1. Preheat oven to 350°F. Remove giblets and neck from goose; reserve for another use. Trim and discard fat from body cavity and any excess skin. Rinse goose inside and out with cold running water; drain well. Pat dry with paper towels. With goose breast side up, lift wings up toward neck, then fold wing tips under back of goose so wings stay in place. With string, tie legs and tail together. Fold neck skin over back. With two-tine fork, prick skin in several places to drain fat during roasting.

2. Place goose, breast side up, on rack in large roasting pan (17" by 11 1/2"). Rub goose with salt, pepper, and ground sage. Roast, spooning off fat from pan occasionally, 3 hours to 3 hours 30 minutes. During last hour of roasting, cover goose with foil to prevent overbrowning, if necessary.

3. Meanwhile, prepare glaze: In small bowl, stir sugar, soy sauce, vinegar, and ginger until blended. After goose has roasted 2 hours 30 minutes, with pastry brush, brush goose with glaze. Continue roasting, brushing goose occasionally with glaze, 30 minutes to 1 hour longer. Goose is done when instant-read thermometer inserted in thickest part of thigh (not next to bone) reaches 180°F. Internal temperature of goose will rise to 185°F upon standing.

4. Transfer goose to warm large platter; keep warm. Let stand 15 minutes to set juices for easier carving. Reserve pan drippings.

5. Prepare gravy: Remove rack from roasting pan. Strain pan drippings through sieve into 8-cup measuring cup or large bowl. Let stand until fat separates from pan juices. Spoon 2 tablespoons fat from drippings into 2-quart saucepan. Skim and reserve remaining fat for another use. Add *1/2 cup water* to roasting pan, stirring until browned bits are loosened from bottom of pan. Add to pan juices in measuring cup. If necessary, add enough *additional water* to pan juices to equal 2 cups.

6. Add flour to fat in saucepan and cook over medium heat; whisking until blended and smooth. Gradually add pan-juice mixture and bouillon; cook, whisking constantly, until mixture thickens slightly and boils. Pour gravy into gravy boat. Serve goose with gravy.

Each serving: About 905 calories, 73g protein, 6g carbohydrate, 63g total fat (20g saturated), 263mg cholesterol, 810mg sodium.

Crispy Roasted Goose with Orange Sauce

Piercing the skin of goose helps drain off the large amount of fat and also crisps the skin. Pour all the flavorful fat through a fine sieve and freeze for up to four months. Use for browning potatoes.

PREP: 30 MINUTES   ROAST: 4 HOURS 25 MINUTES
MAKES 10 MAIN-DISH SERVINGS.

1 goose (12 pounds)
5 navel oranges, each cut in half
1 bunch thyme
4 bay leaves
1/2 teaspoon dried thyme
1 1/4 teaspoons salt

1/2 teaspoon coarsely ground black pepper
3 tablespoons orange-flavored liqueur
2 tablespoons cornstarch
1/2 cup orange marmalade

1. Preheat oven to 400°F. Remove giblets and neck from goose; reserve for another use. Trim and discard fat from body cavity and any excess skin. Rinse goose inside and out with cold running water and drain well; pat dry with paper towels. With goose breast side up, lift wings up toward neck, then fold wing tips under back of goose so wings stay in place. Place 6 orange halves, thyme sprigs, and bay leaves in body cavity. Tie legs and tail together with string. Fold neck skin over back. With two-tine fork, prick skin in several places to drain fat during roasting.

2. Place goose, breast side up, on rack in large roasting pan (17" by 11 1/2"). In cup, combine dried thyme, 1 teaspoon salt, and pepper; rub mixture over goose. Cover goose and roasting pan with foil. Roast 1 hour 30 minutes; turn oven control to 325°F and roast 2 hours longer.

3. Meanwhile, in small bowl, from remaining 4 orange halves, squeeze 3/4 cup juice. Stir in 1 tablespoon liqueur, cornstarch, and the remaining 1/4 teaspoon salt; set aside. In cup, mix orange marmalade with remaining 2 tablespoons liqueur.

4. With spoon or bulb baster, remove as much fat from roasting pan as possible. Remove foil and roast goose 45 minutes longer. Remove goose from oven and turn oven control to 450°F. Brush marmalade mixture

over goose. Roast goose until skin is golden brown and crisp, about 10 minutes longer. Goose is done when instant-read thermometer inserted in thickest part of thigh (not next to bone) reaches 180°F. Internal temperature of goose will rise to 185°F upon standing. Transfer goose to warm platter; let stand at least 15 minutes to set juices for easier carving.

5. Prepare sauce: Remove rack from roasting pan. Strain pan drippings through sieve into 8-cup measuring cup or large bowl. Let stand until fat separates from drippings; skim and reserve fat for another use (there should be about 5 cups fat). Measure pan juices; if necessary, add enough *water* to pan juices to equal 1 cup. Return pan juices to pan and add reserved orange-juice mixture. Heat sauce to boiling over medium heat, stirring; boil 1 minute. (Makes about 1 3/4 cups.) Serve sauce with goose. Remove skin before eating, if desired.

Each serving with skin: About 810 calories, 66g protein, 5g carbohydrate, 57g total fat (18g saturated), 235mg cholesterol, 472mg sodium.

Each serving without skin: About 488 calories, 57g protein, 5g carbohydrate, 25g total fat (9g saturated), 188mg cholesterol, 440mg sodium.

Roast Duck with Cherry-Port Sauce

Made with tart cherries, this sauce is not overly sweet. We accompanied the duck with roasted pears. You could also serve roasted potatoes, Brussels sprouts, or carrots. Make the Giblet Broth while the duck roasts.

PREP: 10 MINUTES PLUS PREPARING BROTH   ROAST: 2 HOURS 30 MINUTES
MAKES 4 MAIN-DISH SERVINGS.

1 duck (4 1/2 pounds), giblets and
   neck reserved for Giblet Broth
1/2 teaspoon dried thyme
1/4 teaspoon salt
1/4 teaspoon ground black pepper
2 Bosc pears, each cut into quarters
   and cored

2 teaspoons sugar
1/4 cup minced shallots
1/3 cup Port wine
1/4 cup dried tart cherries

1. Preheat oven to 350°F. Trim and discard fat from body cavity. Rinse duck inside and out with cold running water; drain well. Pat duck dry with paper towels. Lift wings up toward neck; fold wing tips under back of duck so they stay in place. With two-tine fork, prick skin in several places to drain fat during roasting. Sprinkle 1/4 teaspoon thyme inside body cavity. With string, tie legs and tail together.

2. Place duck, breast side up, on rack in medium roasting pan (14" by 10"). Sprinkle salt, pepper, and remaining 1/4 teaspoon thyme on outside of duck.

3. Roast, occasionally spooning off fat, 2 hours 30 minutes. Duck is done when temperature on meat thermometer inserted in thickest part of thigh, next to body, reaches 180° to 185°F. While duck is roasting, prepare Giblet Broth.

4. After duck has roasted 2 hours, place pears in small baking dish. Sprinkle with sugar; roast until tender, about 30 minutes. Transfer duck and pears to platter; keep warm. Let duck stand 15 minutes to set juices for easier carving.

5. Prepare sauce: Skim and discard fat from drippings in pan. Add shallots to pan; cook over medium-high heat, stirring, 2 minutes. Stir in Port, dried cherries, and giblet broth; heat to boiling, stirring until brown bits

are loosened from bottom of pan. Simmer 5 minutes. Pour into small bowl. Serve duck with Cherry-Port Sauce and roasted pears.

Each serving: About 790 calories, 39g protein, 25g carbohydrate, 57g total fat (19g saturated), 171mg cholesterol, 685mg sodium.

Giblet Broth

In 2-quart saucepan, heat **duck giblets** (except liver) and **neck, 1 can (14 1/2 ounces) chicken broth**, and **2 cups water** to boiling over high heat. Reduce heat to low; simmer, uncovered, 1 hour 30 minutes (if liquid evaporates too quickly, add 1/2 **cup more water**). Pour broth through strainer set over 1-cup measuring cup; discard giblets. Makes 1/2 to 3/4 cup.

TIP: Carving a Roast Duck

1. To remove wing, cut through joint between wing and body. To remove leg, cut through skin around leg, then cut down between thigh and body to reveal joint; cut through joint to separate. Cut drumstick from thigh through center joint. Repeat with second wing and leg.
2. Holding knife blade at a 45° angle, cut long, thin slices from one side of breast. Repeat on other side.

Ginger-Glazed Duck

To ensure crisp, flavorful skin, this glazed duck is roasted at high heat during the last ten minutes.

PREP: 10 MINUTES   ROAST: 2 HOURS 10 MINUTES
MAKES 4 MAIN-DISH SERVINGS.

1 duck (4 1/2 pounds), cut into quarters, fat removed
3 teaspoons grated, peeled fresh ginger

1/2 teaspoon salt
1/4 teaspoon ground black pepper
2 tablespoons honey
1 tablespoon soy sauce

1. Preheat oven to 350°F. Pat duck dry with paper towels. With two-tine fork, prick skin in several places.

2. In cup, combine 1 teaspoon ginger, salt, and pepper; rub on meat side of duck quarters. Place the duck, skin side up, on rack in large (17" by 11 1/2") foil-lined roasting pan. Roast 2 hours, using spoon or bulb baster to remove fat from pan occasionally.

3. Meanwhile, in cup, combine the honey, soy sauce, and the remaining 2 teaspoons ginger.

4. Turn oven control to 450°F. Remove duck from oven and brush all over with ginger glaze. Return to oven and roast 10 minutes longer. Duck is done when temperature on meat thermometer inserted in thickest part of thigh, next to body, reaches 180° to 185°F.

5. Transfer duck to platter and serve.

Each serving: About 690 calories, 37g protein, 9g carbohydrate, 55g total fat (19g saturated), 163mg cholesterol, 662mg sodium.

Spiced Duck

Marinating duck overnight gives it flavor that's hard to match.

PREP: 10 MINUTES PLUS OVERNIGHT TO MARINATE   ROAST: 2 HOURS
MAKES 4 MAIN-DISH SERVINGS.

2 green onions, trimmed and cut into
2-inch pieces
2 teaspoons salt
1 teaspoon crushed red pepper
1 teaspoon fennel seeds, crushed
1/4 teaspoon ground cloves

1/4 teaspoon ground ginger
1 duck (4 1/2 pounds), cut into
quarters, fat removed
1 tablespoon soy sauce
2 tablespoons honey

1. Crush green onions with side of chef's knife. In small bowl, combine salt, crushed red pepper, fennel seeds, cloves, and ginger.

2. Pat duck dry with paper towels. With two-tine fork, prick duck skin in several places.

3. Rub duck quarters with crushed green onions; discard green onions. Rub duck with spice mixture. Place duck in large bowl; cover and refrigerate overnight to marinate.

4. Preheat oven to 350°F. Place duck, skin side up, on rack in large (17" by 11 1/2") roasting pan. Roast 2 hours.

5. About 15 minutes before duck is done, brush with soy sauce, then with honey; continue roasting until golden brown and tender. Duck is done when temperature on meat thermometer inserted in thickest part of duck reaches 180°F to 185°F. Transfer duck pieces to platter and serve.

Each serving: About 695 calories, 37g protein, 10g carbohydrate, 55g total fat (19g saturated), 163mg cholesterol, 1,539mg sodium.

BEEF, VEAL & LAMB

Pepper-Crusted Beef Tenderloin with Red-Wine Gravy

Herb-Crusted Rib Roast

If you like, reserve the fat from the pan drippings to make Yorkshire Pudding (page 113), a traditional accompaniment for roast beef. Or for something simpler, try the crispy Pan-Roasted Potatoes (page 200) which can cook at the same time as the roast.

PREP: 15 MINUTES ROAST: 2 HOURS 30 MINUTES
MAKES 8 MAIN-DISH SERVINGS.

1 (3-rib) beef rib roast from small end (5 1/2 pounds), trimmed and chine bone removed
1 teaspoon salt
1/2 teaspoon dried rosemary, crumbled
1/4 teaspoon ground black pepper
1 lemon

1 1/2 cups fresh bread crumbs (about 3 slices bread)
1/2 cup chopped fresh parsley
2 garlic cloves, finely chopped
1 tablespoon olive oil
2 tablespoons Dijon mustard

1. Preheat oven to 325°F. In medium roasting pan (14" by 10"), place rib roast, fat side up. In small bowl, combine salt, rosemary, and pepper. Use to rub on roast.

2. Roast beef until meat thermometer inserted in thickest part of meat (not touching bone) reaches 135°F, about 2 hours 30 minutes. Internal temperature of meat will rise to 140°F (medium) upon standing. Or roast until desired doneness.

3. About 1 hour before roast is done, prepare bread coating: From lemon, grate 1/2 teaspoon peel and squeeze 1 tablespoon juice. In small bowl, combine lemon peel and juice, bread crumbs, parsley, garlic, and oil. Remove roast from oven; spread mustard on top of roast. Press bread-crumb mixture onto mustard-coated roast. Roast 1 hour longer or until desired doneness.

4. When roast is done, transfer to warm large platter and let stand 15 minutes to set juices for easier carving.

Each serving: About 352 calories, 39g protein, 5g carbohydrate, 18g total fat (7g saturated), 112mg cholesterol, 508mg sodium.

Herb-Crusted Rib Roast

Beef Rib Roast with Creamy Horseradish Sauce

There aren't enough pan drippings from a rib roast to make gravy for ten, so we suggest a zesty horseradish sauce instead.

PREP: 25 MINUTES   ROAST: 3 HOURS   MAKES 10 MAIN-DISH SERVINGS.

1 (4-rib) beef rib roast from small end (7 pounds), trimmed and chine bone removed
3 tablespoons whole tricolor peppercorns (red, green, and black)

1 teaspoon salt
Creamy Horseradish Sauce (page 109)

1. Preheat oven to 325°F. In medium roasting pan (14" by 10"), place rib roast, fat side up. In mortar, with pestle, crush peppercorns with salt. Use to rub on fat side of roast.

2. Roast beef until meat thermometer inserted in thickest part of meat (not touching bone) reaches 135°F, about 3 hours. Internal temperature of rib roast will rise to 140°F (medium-rare) upon standing. Or roast until desired doneness.

3. When roast is done, transfer to warm large platter and let stand 15 minutes to set juices for easier carving. Meanwhile, prepare Creamy Horseradish Sauce.

Each serving without sauce: About 317 calories, 39g protein, 1g carbohydrate, 16g total fat (7g saturated), 113mg cholesterol, 322mg sodium.

Creamy Horseradish Sauce

In small bowl, combine **1 jar (6 ounces) white horseradish**, drained, **1/2 cup mayonnaise**, **1 teaspoon sugar**, and **1/2 teaspoon salt**. Whip **1/2 cup heavy or whipping cream** and fold into horseradish mixture. Makes about 1 2/3 cups.

Each tablespoon: About 49 calories, 0g protein, 1g carbohydrate, 5g total fat (2g saturated), 9mg cholesterol, 74mg sodium.

Shallot-Garlic Rib Roast with Cabernet Gravy

Turn a straightforward rib roast into an elegant entrée with shallots and red wine. The shallots are used to flavor the roast and the gravy is enriched with sautéed shallots as well as red wine.

PREP: 25 MINUTES   ROAST: 2 HOURS 15 MINUTES
MAKES 10 MAIN-DISH SERVINGS.

4 garlic cloves, crushed with press
1 1/2 teaspoons salt
1 teaspoon cracked black pepper
3 large shallots (about 6 ounces), finely chopped (3/4 cup)
1 (3-rib) beef rib roast from small end (5 1/2 pounds), trimmed and chine bone removed

1/2 cup Cabernet Sauvignon or other dry red wine
2 teaspoons all-purpose flour
1 cup chicken broth

1. Preheat oven to 325°F. In small bowl, stir garlic, salt, pepper, and 1/3 cup shallots. Use to rub on roast. (Wrap remaining shallots in plastic wrap and refrigerate to use in gravy.) Place roast, fat side up, in medium roasting pan (14" by 10"). Roast beef until meat thermometer inserted in thickest part of meat (not touching bone) reaches 135°F, 2 hours and 15 minutes. Internal temperature of meat will rise to 140°F (medium-rare) upon standing. Or roast until desired doneness.

2. When roast is done, transfer to warm large platter or cutting board; keep warm. Let stand 15 minutes to set juices for easier carving.

3. Meanwhile, prepare gravy: Spoon 1 tablespoon fat from roasting pan into 2-quart saucepan; skim and discard remaining fat. Add wine to roasting pan and heat to boiling over medium heat, stirring until browned bits are loosened from bottom of pan; boil 1 minute. Remove pan from heat.

4. Heat fat in saucepan over medium-low heat until hot. Add remaining shallots and cook, stirring occasionally, until soft and golden, 4 to 5 minutes. Stir in flour and cook, stirring frequently, until flour is lightly

browned, about 2 minutes. Gradually stir in wine from roasting pan and broth; cook, stirring constantly, until gravy boils and thickens slightly. Remove saucepan from heat. Stir meat juices from platter into gravy. Pour gravy into gravy boat. Makes about 1½ cups gravy. Serve gravy with roast.

Each serving with gravy: About 425 calories, 26g protein, 4g carbohydrate, 33g total fat (13g saturated), 95mg cholesterol, 525mg sodium.

Shallot-Garlic Rib Roast with Cabernet Gravy

Beef Roast with Yorkshire Pudding

This recipe harks back to our founding fathers. To observe tradition, include the Yorkshire Pudding and serve with Madeira gravy.

PREP: 15 MINUTES   ROAST: 3 HOURS
MAKES 12 MAIN-DISH SERVINGS.

1 (3-rib) beef rib roast (7 pounds),
   chine bone removed
1 tablespoon fennel seeds
1 teaspoon coarsely ground
   black pepper
1 teaspoon salt
2 tablespoons chopped fresh parsley

Yorkshire Pudding (optional;
   page 113)
1/4 cup Madeira wine or dry sherry
2 tablespoons all-purpose flour
1 1/4 teaspoons beef-flavor
   instant bouillon

1. Preheat oven to 325°F. Pat roast dry with paper towels. In mortar, with pestle, crush fennel seeds. Stir in pepper, salt, and parsley. Use to rub on roast. Place roast, fat side up, on rack in large roasting pan (17" by 11 1/2").
2. Roast beef until meat thermometer inserted in thickest part of meat (not touching bone) reaches 135°F, about 2 hours 20 minutes. Internal temperature of meat will rise to 140°F (medium-rare) upon standing. Or roast until desired doneness.
3. Transfer beef to warm large platter; keep warm. Let stand 15 minutes to set juices for easier carving. Remove rack from roasting pan. Strain pan drippings through sieve into 2-cup measuring cup. Let stand until fat separates from pan juices, about 1 minute. Spoon 2 tablespoons of the fat into 2-quart saucepan. Skim the remaining fat; discard or reserve for Yorkshire Pudding.
4. Prepare Yorkshire Pudding, if you like.
5. Prepare gravy: Add Madeira and *1/2 cup water* to roasting pan and cook, stirring over medium heat until browned bits are loosened from bottom of pan. Add Madeira mixture to pan juices in measuring cup. Add enough *water* to equal 2 cups if necessary; set aside. Into fat in saucepan, stir flour

until blended; cook over medium heat, stirring constantly, until flour turns golden. Gradually stir in pan-juice mixture and bouillon; cook, stirring, until gravy boils and thickens slightly.

6. Serve gravy with beef and Yorkshire Pudding, if you like.

Each serving: About 530 calories, 70g protein, 1g carbohydrate, 24g total fat (9g saturated), 167mg cholesterol, 320mg sodium.

Yorkshire Pudding

Preheat oven to 450°F. In medium bowl, with wire whisk, beat **3 large eggs**, **1 1/2 cups milk**, **1 1/2 cups all-purpose flour**, and **3/4 teaspoon salt** until smooth. Spoon **3 tablespoons roast-beef pan drippings** into metal baking pan (13" by 9"); place in oven for 2 minutes. Remove pan from oven. Pour milk mixture over hot drippings. Bake until puffed and lightly browned, about 25 minutes. Cut into squares; serve hot. (For individual puddings, use eighteen 2 1/2" by 1 1/2" muffin-pan cups; bake puddings only 12 to 15 minutes.) Makes 12 accompaniment servings.

Each square: 160 calories, 6g protein, 19g carbohydrate, 6g total fat, (3g saturated), 89mg cholesterol, 250mg sodium.

Each muffin: About 71 calories, 3g protein, 8g carbohydrate, 3g total fat (1g saturated), 39mg cholesterol, 110mg sodium.

Black-Pepper Beef Roast with Shallot Sauce

This no-fuss boneless roast just about cooks itself. Serve with the shallot sauce made with pan drippings.

PREP: 25 MINUTES   ROAST: 1 HOUR 15 MINUTES
MAKES 10 MAIN-DISH SERVINGS.

1 boneless beef rib-eye roast
  (3 pounds), tied
1 tablespoon plus 1 teaspoon
  cracked black pepper
1 tablespoon olive oil

1 teaspoon salt
1 medium shallot, minced (1/4 cup)
1 can (14 1/2 ounces) beef broth

1. Preheat oven to 350°F. Place beef on rack in medium roasting pan (14" by 10").
2. In small bowl, stir pepper, oil, and salt until blended. Use to rub on roast.
3. Roast beef until meat thermometer inserted in the thickest part of meat reaches 135°F, about 1 hour and 15 minutes. Internal temperature of meat will rise to 140°F (medium-rare) upon standing. Or roast to desired doneness. Transfer roast to large platter; keep warm. Let stand 10 minutes to set juices for easier slicing.
4. Meanwhile, prepare Shallot Sauce: Spoon 2 tablespoons fat from roasting pan into 10-inch skillet; skim and discard remaining fat. Add shallot to fat in skillet and cook, stirring frequently, over medium heat until tender and lightly browned, 3 to 5 minutes.
5. Add broth to roasting pan and cook over medium-high heat, stirring until browned bits are loosened from bottom of pan, about 2 minutes. Add broth mixture to skillet and heat to boiling over high heat; boil until sauce is slightly reduced, about 3 minutes. Pour into sauceboat and keep warm.
6. To serve, remove string from roast and cut into thin slices. Serve roast with Shallot Sauce.

Each serving without sauce: About 330 calories, 26g protein, 1g carbohydrate, 24g total fat (9g saturated), 85mg cholesterol, 300mg sodium.

Each tablespoon sauce: About 10 calories, 0g protein, 0g carbohydrate, 1g total fat (1g saturated), 1mg cholesterol, 55mg sodium.

Beef Eye Round au Jus

Roast some herbed new potatoes at the same time. And for the tenderest results, do not roast this cut to more than medium-rare.

PREP: 30 MINUTES   ROAST: 1 HOUR 10 MINUTES
MAKES 12 MAIN-DISH SERVINGS.

1¹/₂ teaspoons salt
¹/₂ teaspoon dried thyme
¹/₄ teaspoon ground black pepper
1 beef eye round roast
  (4¹/₂ pounds), trimmed
2 tablespoons olive oil
1 bag (16 ounces) carrots, peeled
  and cut into 2" by
  ¹/₄" matchstick strips

1 pound leeks (3 medium), white and
  light green parts, cut into
  2" by ¹/₄" matchstick strips
4 garlic cloves, thinly sliced
1¹/₄ cups dry red wine
¹/₂ cup water
1 bay leaf

1. Preheat oven to 450°F. In small bowl, combine salt, thyme, and pepper. Use to rub on roast. In 10-inch skillet, heat oil over medium-high heat until very hot. Add beef and cook until browned, about 10 minutes. Transfer beef to nonreactive medium roasting pan (14" by 10").

2. Add carrots, leeks, and garlic to skillet and cook, stirring occasionally, until carrots are tender, about 7 minutes. Arrange vegetable mixture around beef.

3. Roast beef 25 minutes. Add wine, water, and bay leaf to roasting pan. Turn oven control to 325°F and roast until meat thermometer inserted in center of meat reaches 135°F, about 45 minutes longer. Internal temperature of meat will rise to 140°F (medium-rare) upon standing. Or roast until desired doneness. Remove and discard bay leaf.

4. When roast is done, transfer to warm large platter; keep warm. Let stand 15 minutes to set juices for easier slicing.

5. To serve, cut roast into thin slices and serve with vegetables.

Each serving: About 232 calories, 33g protein, 6g carbohydrate, 8g total fat (2g saturated), 76mg cholesterol, 358mg sodium.

Pepper-Crusted Beef Tenderloin with Red-Wine Gravy

A simple black-pepper crust highlights this elegant piece of meat. When shopping for a whole tenderloin, don't be surprised that it weighs up to 6 pounds before it's trimmed down to its roasting weight of 4 1/2 pounds. If possible, ask the butcher to do it for you. If tying the roast yourself, make sure to tuck the thin, narrow end under so the tenderloin cooks evenly.

PREP: 30 MINUTES   ROAST: 50 MINUTES
MAKES 10 MAIN-DISH SERVINGS.

TENDERLOIN ROAST
3 tablespoons cracked black pepper
1 tablespoon olive oil
1 teaspoon salt
1 whole beef tenderloin
(4 1/2 pounds), trimmed and tied

RED-WINE GRAVY
2 tablespoons butter or margarine
4 medium shallots (6 ounces),
minced (1/2 cup)
1 can (14 1/2 ounces) chicken broth
1 cup dry red wine
1/2 cup loosely packed fresh parsley
leaves, chopped

1. Prepare roast: Preheat oven to 425°F. In cup, mix pepper, olive oil, and salt. Use to rub on meat. Place tenderloin on rack in large roasting pan (17" by 11 1/2"). Roast tenderloin until meat thermometer inserted in center of meat reaches 135°F, about 50 minutes. Internal temperature of the tenderloin will rise to 140°F (medium-rare) upon standing. Or roast to desired doneness.

2. About 20 minutes before tenderloin is done, prepare gravy: In 2-quart saucepan, melt butter over medium heat. Add shallots and cook until tender and golden, stirring often, about 10 minutes. Add broth and wine and heat to boiling over high heat; boil until the sauce is reduced to about 2 1/3 cups, about 10 minutes. Remove pan from heat.

3. When tenderloin is done, transfer to large platter; keep warm. Let stand 10 minutes to set juices for easier slicing.

4. Meanwhile, remove rack from roasting pan. Skim and discard fat from drippings in pan.

Pepper-Crusted Beef Tenderloin with Red-Wine Gravy

5. To serve, add pan juices and any meat juice on platter to gravy; heat through. Stir in chopped parsley.

6. Remove string from tenderloin and cut into thin slices. Serve tenderloin with gravy.

Each serving without gravy: About 360 calories, 43g protein, 1g carbohydrate, 19g total fat (7g saturated), 127mg cholesterol, 310mg sodium.

Each ¼ cup gravy: About 40 calories, 1g protein, 2g carbohydrate, 3g total fat (2g saturated), 6mg cholesterol, 158mg sodium.

Roast Beef with Caper Sauce

This herb-rubbed beef roast comes with a lively caper sauce that requires no cooking.

PREP: 25 MINUTES PLUS STANDING   ROAST: 1 HOUR 30 MINUTES
MAKES 8 MAIN-DISH SERVINGS.

1 beef eye round roast
   (4 pounds), trimmed
2 teaspoons dried thyme
1 teaspoon ground sage
4 garlic cloves, minced
1/4 teaspoons salt
2 teaspoons coarsely ground
   black pepper

3/4 cup olive or vegetable oil
1/2 cup capers, drained and chopped
1/3 cup Dijon mustard
1 tablespoon chopped fresh chives
1/4 cup water

1. Preheat oven to 325°F. Pat roast dry with paper towels. In cup, mix thyme, sage, garlic, salt, and 1 1/4 teaspoons pepper. Use to rub on roast. Place roast on rack in small roasting pan (13" by 9").

2. Roast beef until meat thermometer inserted in thickest part of the meat reaches 135°F, about 1 hour 30 minutes. Internal temperature of meat will rise to 140°F (medium-rare) upon standing. Or roast until desired doneness. Transfer roast to warm large platter; let stand 15 minutes to set juices for easier slicing.

3. Meanwhile, prepare sauce: In small bowl, mix the oil, capers, mustard, chives, remaining 3/4 teaspoon pepper, and the water until blended. Makes about 2 cups.

4. To serve, cut roast into thin slices. Serve with Caper Sauce.

Each serving: About 730 calories, 44g protein, 5g carbohydrate, 59g total fat (16g saturated), 153mg cholesterol, 1,055mg sodium.

Asian Beef Tenderloin

Here's an easy and flavorful roast. Simply put the spices in a ziptight plastic bag, add the tenderloin and let it marinate as long as overnight. Then pop the meat in the oven and let it roast.

PREP: 10 MINUTES PLUS MARINATING   ROAST: 50 TO 60 MINUTES
MAKES 16 MAIN-DISH SERVINGS.

1/2 cup soy sauce
3 tablespoons grated, peeled
  fresh ginger
1 1/2 teaspoons fennel seeds, crushed
1/2 teaspoon crushed red pepper

1/2 teaspoon cracked black pepper
1/4 teaspoon ground cloves
1 beef tenderloin roast
  (5 pounds), tied
1 tablespoon vegetable oil

1. In large ziptight plastic bag, mix soy sauce, ginger, fennel seeds, crushed red pepper, black pepper, and cloves. Add tenderloin, turning to coat with marinade. Seal bag securely, pressing out as much air as possible, and place in large baking dish or roasting pan. Refrigerate tenderloin 6 hours, or overnight, turning bag occasionally.

2. Preheat oven to 425°F. Place tenderloin on rack in large roasting pan (17" by 11 1/2"); discard marinade. Brush tenderloin with oil. Roast tenderloin until meat thermometer inserted in center of meat reaches 135°F, 50 to 60 minutes. Internal temperature of meat will rise to 140°F (medium-rare) upon standing. Or roast until desired doneness.

3. Transfer tenderloin to cutting board; keep warm. Let stand 10 minutes to set juices for easier slicing.

4. To serve, cut tenderloin into thin slices.

Each serving: About 225 calories, 31g protein, 0g carbohydrate, 10g total fat (4g saturated), 74mg cholesterol, 195mg sodium.

Mushroom-Stuffed Beef Tenderloin

Three types of mushrooms—porcini, shiitake, and white—add up to an especially rich and delicious stuffing. Slathered with mushroom gravy—this impressive roast makes great party fare!

PREP: 1 HOUR 30 MINUTES   ROAST: 1 HOUR
MAKES 10 MAIN-DISH SERVINGS.

MUSHROOM STUFFING

1 1/2 cups boiling water
1 package (0.5 ounce) sliced dried
    porcini mushrooms (about 1/2 cup)
4 tablespoons butter or margarine
2 slices white bread, torn into
    small pieces
1/2 cup loosely packed fresh parsley
    leaves, chopped
1 tablespoon olive oil
12 ounces shiitake mushrooms,
    stems removed and caps
    coarsely chopped
10 ounces white mushrooms,
    trimmed and sliced
4 large shallots (about 8 ounces),
    minced (about 1 cup)
3/4 teaspoon salt
1/4 teaspoon dried thyme
1/4 cup brandy (optional)

BEEF TENDERLOIN

1 tablespoon olive oil
1 teaspoon salt
1 teaspoon coarsely ground
    black pepper
1 teaspoon dried thyme
1 whole beef tenderloin (4 to
    4 1/2 pounds), trimmed

MUSHROOM GRAVY

2 tablespoons brandy or water
1 can (14 1/2 ounces) chicken broth
    (1 3/4 cups)
reserved soaking liquid from
    porcini mushrooms
1 tablespoon butter or margarine
10 ounces white mushrooms,
    trimmed and sliced
2 tablespoons all-purpose flour

1. Prepare stuffing: In small bowl, pour boiling water over dried porcini; let stand 30 minutes.

2. Meanwhile, in 12-inch skillet, melt 2 tablespoons butter over medium heat. Add bread and cook, stirring occasionally, until toasted and golden, about 5 minutes. Transfer bread to medium bowl; stir in parsley.

3. In same skillet, heat oil and remaining 2 tablespoons butter over medium-high heat. Add shiitake mushrooms and white mushrooms and cook until mushrooms are golden and liquid has evaporated, 12 to 15 minutes.

Add shallots, salt, and thyme and cook, stirring occasionally, 5 minutes longer. Stir in brandy; cook 1 minute longer. Remove skillet from heat; stir in half of bread mixture. Let stuffing cool.

4. With slotted spoon, remove porcini from soaking liquid; reserve liquid. Rinse porcini to remove any grit, then chop. Add chopped porcini to mushroom mixture in skillet. Strain porcini soaking liquid through sieve lined with paper towel; reserve for gravy.

5. Prepare tenderloin: In cup, mix oil, salt, pepper, and thyme. Use to rub on tenderloin. Turn thinner end of meat under tenderloin for even thickness. Using sharp knife, cut 1 1/2-inch-deep lengthwise slit in tenderloin, beginning 2 inches from the thicker end and ending 2 inches from the thinner end.

6. Preheat oven to 425°F. Spoon cooled stuffing into slit in tenderloin. Tie with string at 2 inch intervals to secure. Place stuffed tenderloin on rack in large roasting pan (17" by 11 1/2"); roast until meat thermometer inserted in center of tenderloin reaches 135°F, about 1 hour. Internal temperature of meat will rise to 140°F (medium-rare) upon standing. Or roast to desired doneness.

7. Remove tenderloin from oven; sprinkle remaining bread mixture over stuffing. Roast tenderloin until bread topping is golden, about 5 minutes longer. Transfer tenderloin to large platter; keep warm. Let stand 10 minutes to set juices for easier slicing.

8. Meanwhile prepare gravy: To drippings in roasting pan, add brandy, 1/2 cup broth, and 1/2 cup reserved porcini soaking liquid and cook over low heat, stirring until browned bits are loosened from bottom of pan. Pour drippings through sieve into 4-cup measuring cup. Let stand until fat separates from pan juices, about 1 minute. Skim and discard fat. Add remaining broth and enough porcini soaking liquid to equal 2 1/2 cups total; set aside.

9. In 12-inch skillet, melt butter over medium-high heat. Add mushrooms and cook, stirring, until mushrooms are golden and liquid has evaporated, about 10 minutes. Stir in flour; cook 1 minute, stirring. Gradually stir pan-juice mixture into mushrooms and cook, stirring constantly, until gravy boils and thickens slightly; boil 1 minute.

10. To serve, remove string from tenderloin and cut into thin slices. Serve with gravy.

Each serving: About 490 calories, 46g protein, 14g carbohydrate, 27g total fat (11g saturated), 142mg cholesterol, 767mg sodium.

Spinach-Stuffed Tenderloin with Mushroom Gravy

A real showstopper. We gild the lily by dressing up this already exquisite roast with a melt-in-your-mouth stuffing.

PREP: 45 MINUTES ROAST/COOK: 1 HOUR
MAKES 10 MAIN-DISH SERVINGS.

Spinach-Mushroom Stuffing (page 123)
2 teaspoons chopped fresh thyme
1 teaspoon salt
1 teaspoon coarsely ground black pepper
1 whole beef tenderloin, trimmed (4 pounds)

2 tablespoons butter or margarine
1/4 cup plain dried bread crumbs
1 can (14 1/2 ounces) chicken broth
2 tablespoons dry vermouth
8 ounces mushrooms, trimmed and sliced
2 tablespoons all-purpose flour

1. Prepare Spinach-Mushroom Stuffing; set aside.
2. Preheat oven to 425°F. In small bowl, combine thyme, salt, and pepper; use to rub on tenderloin. Turn thinner end of meat under tenderloin to make meat an even thickness. With sharp knife, cut 1 1/2-inch-deep slit in tenderloin, beginning 2 inches from thicker end of meat and ending 2 inches from opposite end.
3. Spoon stuffing into slit in tenderloin. With string, tie at 2-inch intervals to secure. Place the stuffed tenderloin on rack in large roasting pan (17" by 11 1/2"); roast 30 minutes.
4. Meanwhile, in 1-quart saucepan, melt 1 tablespoon butter over low heat. Remove saucepan from heat; stir in bread crumbs.
5. Remove tenderloin from oven; sprinkle bread-crumb topping on stuffing. Roast tenderloin until meat thermometer inserted in center of meat reaches 135°F, about 10 minutes longer. Internal temperature of meat will rise to 140°F (medium-rare) upon standing. Or roast until desired doneness.
6. Transfer tenderloin to warm platter; keep warm. Let stand 10 minutes to set juices for easier slicing.

7. Meanwhile, prepare mushroom gravy: Add 1/2 cup broth and vermouth to drippings in roasting pan and cook over low heat, stirring until browned bits are loosened from bottom of pan. Pour drippings mixture into 4-cup measuring cup; let stand until fat separates from pan juices. Skim and discard fat from pan-juice mixture. Add remaining broth and enough *water* to equal 2 1/2 cups; set aside.

8. In 12-inch skillet, melt remaining 1 tablespoon butter over medium-high heat. Add mushrooms and cook, stirring occasionally, until golden and liquid has evaporated, about 12 minutes. Stir in flour. Gradually stir pan-juice mixture into mushrooms and cook, stirring constantly, until gravy has thickened slightly and boils; boil 1 minute.

9. To serve, remove string from tenderloin. Cut meat into thin slices and serve with mushroom gravy.

Each serving with gravy: About 371 calories, 35g protein, 8g carbohydrate, 21g total fat (10g saturated), 114mg cholesterol, 679mg sodium.

Spinach-Mushroom Stuffing

In 12-inch skillet, melt **4 tablespoons butter or margarine** over medium-high heat. Add **1 pound mushrooms**, trimmed and coarsely chopped, and cook until golden and liquid has evaporated, 12 to 15 minutes. Stir in **2 tablespoons dry vermouth**; cook 1 minute longer. Remove skillet from heat; stir in **1 package (10 ounces) frozen chopped spinach**, thawed and squeezed dry, **2 tablespoons freshly grated Parmesan cheese, 2 tablespoons plain dried bread crumbs, 1 teaspoon chopped fresh thyme, 1/4 teaspoon salt**, and **1/2 teaspoon coarsely ground black pepper**. Cool.

Deviled Short Ribs

Short ribs have a succulence that can only come from slow, patient cooking. Save this recipe for a leisurely weekend and indulge.

PREP: 10 MINUTES PLUS MARINATING   ROAST: 2 HOURS 45 MINUTES
MAKES 6 MAIN-DISH SERVINGS.

6 tablespoons spicy brown mustard
2 tablespoons cider vinegar
2 tablespoons green jalapeño chile sauce
2 teaspoons Worcestershire sauce

4 pounds beef chuck short ribs
$^3/_4$ teaspoon ground black pepper
1$^1/_2$ cups fresh bread crumbs (about 3 slices bread)

1. In small bowl, combine 3 tablespoons mustard, vinegar, 1 tablespoon jalapeño sauce, and Worcestershire; with wire whisk, whisk until blended. Transfer to ziptight plastic bag; add short ribs, turning to coat. Seal bag, pressing out as much air as possible. Refrigerate ribs at least 1 hour or up to 24 hours to marinate.

2. Preheat oven to 425°F. Arrange ribs on rack in medium roasting pan (14" by 10"). Brush with remaining marinade from bag; roast 40 minutes. Turn oven control to 325°F and roast 1 hour 20 minutes longer.

3. In small bowl, combine remaining 3 tablespoons mustard, remaining 1 tablespoon jalapeño sauce, and black pepper. Brush on top of ribs. Press bread crumbs onto coated ribs; roast until crumbs are crisp and lightly browned, about 45 minutes longer.

Each serving: About 762 calories, 34g protein, 6g carbohydrate, 64g total fat (27g saturated), 143mg cholesterol, 400mg sodium.

Veal Rib Roast

This is company fare at its best. Serve with roasted new potatoes and steamed asparagus.

PREP: 10 MINUTES   ROAST: 2 HOURS   MAKES 8 MAIN-DISH SERVINGS.

1¼ teaspoons salt
½ teaspoon dried sage
¼ teaspoon dried thyme, crumbled
1 tablespoon olive oil
1 veal rib roast (5 pounds), trimmed
  and chine bone removed
4 garlic cloves, not peeled

½ cup white wine
1½ cups chicken broth
1½ teaspoons cornstarch
1 tablespoon water
2 tablespoons fresh lemon juice
1 tablespoon cold butter or margarine

1. Preheat oven to 450°F. In small bowl, combine salt, sage, thyme, and oil. Use to rub on roast. Place veal and garlic in medium roasting pan (14" by 10"). Roast 1 hour.

2. Pour wine into roasting pan, cover veal with loose tent of foil, and turn oven control to 350°F. Roast veal until meat thermometer inserted in thickest part of roast (not touching bone) reaches 155°F, about 1 hour longer. Internal temperature of veal roast will rise to 160°F (medium) upon standing.

3. Transfer roast to cutting board; keep warm. Let stand 15 minutes to set juices for easier carving.

4. Skim and discard fat from drippings in roasting pan; pour any pan juices into 2-quart saucepan. Add broth to roasting pan and heat to boiling, stirring until browned bits are loosened from bottom of pan; add to saucepan. Heat to boiling over medium heat. In small bowl, blend cornstarch with water until smooth. Stir cornstarch mixture into saucepan and heat to boiling over high heat, stirring; boil 1 minute. Remove from heat; stir in lemon juice and swirl in butter. Slice veal and serve with sauce.

Each serving: About 277 calories, 35g protein, 2g carbohydrate, 13g total fat (4g saturated), 159mg cholesterol, 696mg sodium.

Veal Roast with Rosemary & Garlic

We roast this veal shoulder the classic way on a bed of chopped carrot and onion, which add extra flavor to the pan gravy.

PREP: 20 MINUTES   ROAST: 2 HOURS   MAKES 8 MAIN-DISH SERVINGS.

3 garlic cloves, minced
1 teaspoon dried rosemary
1/2 teaspoon dried thyme
1 teaspoon salt
1/2 teaspoon ground black pepper
1 rolled boneless veal shoulder roast
   (3 pounds), tied

1 tablespoon olive oil
1 small onion, finely chopped
1 medium carrot, finely chopped
1/2 cup dry white wine

1. Preheat oven to 350°F. On cutting board, mash garlic, rosemary, thyme, salt, and pepper to a paste. Pat veal dry with paper towels. Rub paste on the veal.

2. In oven-safe 10-inch skillet (if skillet is not oven-safe, wrap handle of skillet with double layer of foil), heat oil over medium-high heat. Add the veal and cook until browned all over, about 10 minutes. Add chopped onion and carrot and place veal on top. Pour in wine.

3. Transfer skillet to oven and roast veal, basting with pan juices every 30 minutes and adding *1/2 cup water* if skillet is dry, until temperature on meat thermometer inserted in center of roast reaches 160°F for medium, about 2 hours.

4. Transfer veal to warm large platter; keep warm. Let stand 10 minutes to set juices for easier carving.

5. Meanwhile, add *3/4 cup water* to same skillet and heat to boiling, stirring until browned bits are loosened from bottom of skillet; simmer 2 minutes. Skim and discard fat from pan. Strain pan juices and vegetables through coarse sieve into medium bowl, pressing hard on vegetables; discard chopped vegetables. Cut veal into thin slices and serve with pan juices.

Each serving: About 205 calories, 27g protein, 3g carbohydrate, 8g total fat (3g saturated), 112mg cholesterol, 365mg sodium.

Stuffed Breast of Veal with Escarole Stuffing

A sumptous meal, ask your butcher to crack bones for easier carving.

PREP: 30 MINUTES PLUS COOLING   ROAST: 2 HOURS
MAKES 6 MAIN-DISH SERVINGS.

2 cans (14 1/2 ounces each) reduced-
   sodium chicken broth
1/2 cup parboiled rice
2 tablespoons olive oil
1 medium onion, diced
1 large stalk celery, diced
1 small head escarole (about
   12 ounces), chopped

1/4 cup dark seedless raisins,
   chopped
1 1/4 teaspoons rubbed sage
1/2 teaspoon salt
1/2 teaspoon ground pepper
1 veal breast (6 pounds) with pocket
   for stuffing
1/2 cup water

1. Prepare stuffing: In 1-quart saucepan, heat 1 1/3 cups broth to boiling over high heat; stir in rice. Reduce heat to low; cover and simmer until rice is tender and all liquid has been absorbed, about 20 minutes.

2. Meanwhile, in 12-inch skillet, heat 1 tablespoon oil over medium-high heat. Add onion and celery; cook, stirring occasionally, until lightly browned. Add escarole; cook, stirring until escarole just wilts. Remove from heat; stir in rice, raisins, and 1/4 teaspoon sage, 1/4 teaspoon salt, and 1/4 teaspoon pepper. Cool to room temperature.

3. Preheat oven to 350°F. Spoon stuffing into pocket of veal; skewer closed if necessary. Place veal, meat side up, in roasting pan. In cup, mix remaining 1 tablespoon oil with remaining 1 teaspoon sage, 1/4 teaspoon salt, and 1/4 teaspoon pepper. Use to rub on veal. Roast veal 1 hour. Pour remaining broth into roasting pan. Roast, basting often, until tender when pierced with tip of knife, and temperature on meat thermometer inserted in center of roast reaches 160°, about 1 hour longer.

4. Transfer to platter; keep warm. Let stand 15 minutes for easier carving.

5. Strain pan drippings through sieve into 2-quart saucepan. Let stand until fat separates from pan juices, about 1 minute. Skim and discard fat. Add water to hot roasting pan and heat to boiling, stirring until browned bits have loosened from bottom of pan; add to pan juices in saucepan and heat through. Serve veal with sauce.

Each serving: About 455 calories, 48g protein, 23g carbohydrate, 18g total fat (4g saturated), 193mg cholesterol, 435mg sodium.

Stuffed Veal Roast Italian Style

Pancetta, unsmoked Italian bacon, lends rich flavor to this roast. If you can't find it, use the mildest regular bacon available.

PREP: 15 MINUTES   ROAST: 1 HOUR 20 MINUTES
MAKES 8 MAIN-DISH SERVINGS.

3 ounces pancetta, chopped
1 shallot, finely chopped
1/4 cup plus 1 tablespoon water
1 package (10 ounces) frozen
  chopped spinach, thawed and
  squeezed dry
3 ounces Fontina cheese, chopped
  (3/4 cup)

1 boneless veal shoulder roast
  (3 pounds)
1/2 cup dry white wine
2 tablespoons heavy or
  whipping cream
3/4 cup chicken broth
3/4 teaspoon cornstarch

1. Preheat oven to 425°F. In 10-inch skillet, combine pancetta, shallot, and 1/4 cup water; heat to boiling over medium heat. Reduce heat and simmer until pancetta is cooked through and shallot is soft, about 5 minutes. Stir in spinach until well combined. Transfer spinach mixture to medium bowl and stir in Fontina until combined.

2. Using sharp knife, cut roast lengthwise three-quarters of the way through, being careful not to cut all the way through. Open and spread flat like a book. Spoon spinach mixture on roast, leaving 1/2-inch border all around. Roll up roast from one long side to enclose filling; tie with string at 1-inch intervals to secure.

3. Place roast in small roasting pan (13" by 9") and roast 30 minutes. Turn oven control to 350°F and roast until meat thermometer inserted in center of roast reaches 155°F, about 50 minutes longer. Internal temperature of meat will rise to 160°F (medium) upon standing. Transfer roast to warm large platter and let stand 15 minutes to set juices for easier slicing.

4. Meanwhile, skim and discard fat from roasting pan. Add wine and heat to boiling, stirring until browned bits are loosened from bottom of pan.

Pour into 1-quart saucepan and heat to boiling. Add cream and heat to boiling; boil until liquid has reduced by half. Add broth and heat to boiling again. In small bowl, blend cornstarch with 1 tablespoon water until smooth. Stir cornstarch mixture into saucepan. Heat to boiling over high heat, stirring. Slice veal and serve with sauce.

Each serving: About 329 calories, 39g protein, 2g carbohydrate, 17g total fat (7g saturated), 173mg cholesterol, 446mg sodium.

**Using a sharp knife, cut roast lengthwise
three quarters of the way through.**

Open roast and spread flat like a book.

Fruit-Stuffed Veal Roast

If you like, use only one type of dried fruit, such as apples, pears, or prunes in the stuffing.

PREP: 35 MINUTES   ROAST: 1 HOUR 20 MINUTES
MAKES 8 MAIN-DISH SERVINGS.

2 slices firm white bread, cut into 1/2-inch cubes	1/2 teaspoon dried rosemary, crumbled
4 teaspoons olive oil	1 boneless veal shoulder roast (2 1/2 pounds)
2 shallots, finely chopped	
1 garlic clove, finely chopped	1/2 cup chicken broth
1/2 cup mixed dried fruit, coarsely chopped	1 Golden Delicious apple, peeled, cored, and chopped
2 teaspoons Dijon mustard	1/4 cup applejack brandy or Calvados
3/4 teaspoon salt	1/2 cup heavy or whipping cream

1. Preheat oven to 375°F. Place bread cubes on cookie sheet and bake until lightly browned, about 5 minutes. Transfer to medium bowl. Turn oven control to 425°F.

2. In 1-quart saucepan, heat 2 teaspoons oil over medium heat. Add half of shallots and the garlic and cook, stirring, until shallot is tender, about 4 minutes; add to bowl with croutons. Add dried fruit, mustard, 1/4 teaspoon salt, and 1/4 teaspoon rosemary; toss to combine.

3. Using sharp knife, cut roast lengthwise three-quarters of the way through, being careful not to cut all the way through. Open and spread flat like a book. Spoon fruit mixture on roast, leaving 1-inch border all around. Roll up roast from one long side to enclose filling; tie with string at 1-inch intervals to secure. Rub 1/4 teaspoon salt and the remaining 1/4 teaspoon rosemary on veal. Place roast in small roasting pan (13" by 9") and roast until lightly browned, about 30 minutes. Turn oven control to 375°F and roast until meat thermometer inserted in center of roast reaches 155°F, about 50 minutes longer. Internal temperature of meat will rise to 160°F (medium) upon standing.

4. Transfer roast to warm platter and let stand 15 minutes to set juices for easier slicing.

5. Meanwhile, skim and discard fat from roasting pan. Add broth and heat to boiling, stirring until browned bits are loosened from bottom of pan. Heat remaining 2 teaspoons oil in skillet over medium heat. Add remaining shallots and cook mixture, stirring frequently, until tender, about 4 minutes. Add apple and cook, stirring frequently, until tender-crisp, about 4 minutes. Remove from heat and add applejack. Return to heat and cook until liquid has evaporated. Add broth from roasting pan and heat to boiling; boil 3 minutes. Add cream and boil until sauce has slightly thickened, about 5 minutes. Stir in remaining 1/4 teaspoon salt.

6. Slice veal and serve with applejack sauce.

Each serving: About 323 calories, 30g protein, 13g carbohydrate, 15g total fat (7g saturated), 145mg cholesterol, 463mg sodium.

Rosemary Leg of Lamb

The French often roast lamb that has first been rubbed with a mix of fragrant dried herbs. We like to do it, too.

PREP: 5 MINUTES ROAST: 1 HOUR 45 MINUTES TO 2 HOURS
MAKES 10 MAIN-DISH SERVINGS.

1 whole bone-in lamb leg (7 1/2 pounds), trimmed
1/2 teaspoon dried rosemary, crumbled

1/2 teaspoon dried thyme, crumbled
1/2 teaspoon salt
1/4 teaspoon ground black pepper

1. Preheat oven to 450°F. Place lamb in large roasting pan (17" by 11 1/2"). In cup, combine rosemary, thyme, salt, and pepper. Use to rub on lamb.
2. Roast lamb 15 minutes. Turn oven control to 350°F and roast, basting every 15 minutes with pan juices, until meat thermometer inserted in thickest part of lamb (not touching bone) reaches 140°F, 1 hour 30 to 45 minutes longer. Internal temperature of meat will rise to 145°F (medium) upon standing. Or roast until desired doneness.
3. When lamb is done, transfer to cutting board; keep warm. Let stand 15 minutes to set juices for easier carving.
4. Carve lamb into slices and arrange on warm platter.

Each serving: About 312 calories, 46g protein, 0g carbohydrate, 13g total fat (5g saturated), 145mg cholesterol, 227mg sodium.

Lamb Roasted over Potatoes

Just add a green vegetable or salad and dinner is done.

PREP: 15 MINUTES   ROAST: 1 HOUR 30 TO 45 MINUTES
MAKES 8 MAIN-DISH SERVINGS.

1 tablespoon butter or margarine
2 medium onions, sliced
1¹/₂ cups chicken broth
3 pounds all-purpose potatoes,
  peeled and thinly sliced
1 teaspoon salt

¹/₂ teaspoon ground black pepper
1 teaspoon olive oil
1 garlic clove, minced
¹/₂ teaspoon dried thyme
1 lamb leg, shank half (3¹/₂ pounds)

1. Preheat oven to 425°F. In 10-inch skillet, melt butter over medium heat. Add onions; cook, stirring frequently, until tender. Stir in broth; heat to boiling over high heat. Remove from heat. In medium roasting pan (14" by 10"), toss potatoes with the onion mixture, ¹/₂ teaspoon salt, and ¹/₄ teaspoon pepper; spread evenly in pan. Roast 15 minutes.

2. Meanwhile, in cup, combine olive oil, garlic, thyme, remaining ¹/₂ teaspoon salt, and remaining ¹/₄ teaspoon pepper. Use to rub on lamb. Stir potatoes; place lamb on top. Roast, stirring potatoes every 20 minutes, until meat thermometer inserted in thickest part of lamb (not touching bone) reaches 140°F, 1 hour to 1 hour 15 minutes longer. Internal temperature of meat will rise to 145°F (medium) upon standing.

3. Transfer lamb to warm large platter; keep warm. Let stand 15 minutes. (If potatoes are not yet tender, roast 15 minutes longer.)

4. Thinly slice lamb; serve with potatoes.

Each serving: About 435 calories, 46g protein, 35g carbohydrate, 12g total fat (5g saturated), 140 mg cholesterol, 585mg sodium.

Roasted Leg of Lamb with Pistachio-Mint Crust

To prevent the nut crust from burning, don't spread it over the roast until after it has cooked for one hour. Some Indian markets sell shelled pistachios, or simply shell your own.

PREP: 30 MINUTES ROAST: 2 HOURS 15 TO 30 MINUTES
MAKES 10 MAIN-DISH SERVINGS.

1 whole bone-in lamb leg
  (7 pounds), trimmed
2 large garlic cloves, sliced
1 1/2 teaspoons salt
2 tablespoons butter or margarine
1 small onion, chopped
1 1/2 slices firm white bread, torn into
  1/4-inch pieces

1/2 cup pistachios, finely chopped
2 tablespoons coarsely chopped
  fresh mint
1/4 teaspoon coarsely ground black
  pepper
1/2 cup Port wine
3 tablespoons all-purpose flour
1 can (14 1/2 ounces) chicken broth

1. Preheat oven to 325°F. Cut about a dozen 1/2-inch-long slits in lamb and insert slice of garlic in each. Sprinkle lamb with 1 teaspoon salt. Place lamb, fat side up, on rack in large roasting pan (17" by 11 1/2"). Roast lamb 1 hour.

2. Meanwhile, in 10-inch skillet, melt butter over medium heat. Add onion and cook until lightly browned and tender, about 10 minutes; remove from heat. Stir in bread, pistachios, mint, remaining 1/2 teaspoon salt, and pepper. After lamb has roasted 1 hour, carefully pat mixture onto the lamb.

3. Roast lamb until meat thermometer inserted in thickest part of lamb (not touching bone) reaches 140°F, 1 hour 15 to 30 minutes longer. Internal temperature of meat will rise to 145°F (medium) upon standing. Or roast until desired doneness.

4. When lamb is done, transfer to warm platter; keep warm. Let stand 15 minutes to set juices for easier carving.

5. Meanwhile, prepare gravy: Remove rack from roasting pan; pour pan drippings into 2-cup measuring cup. Add Port to hot roasting pan and heat to boiling, stirring until browned bits are loosened from bottom of pan; add to drippings in cup. Let stand until fat separates from pan juices, about 1 minute. Skim 2 tablespoons fat from drippings; return to roasting pan. Skim and discard any remaining fat.

6. Heat fat in roasting pan over medium-high heat; stir in flour until well blended. Gradually whisk in pan juices and broth and cook, whisking, until gravy has thickened slightly and boils; boil 1 minute. Pour gravy into gravy boat and serve with lamb.

Each serving: About 404 calories, 46g protein, 8g carbohydrate, 18g total fat (7g saturated), 144mg cholesterol, 680mg sodium.

Onion-Stuffed Butterflied Leg of Lamb

We added wine to the pan juices to make an easy and delicious gravy.

Prep: 20 minutes   Roast: 1 hour 45 minutes
Makes 10 main-dish servings.

4 tablespoons butter or margarine
1 large onion (12 ounces), minced
1 garlic clove, minced
salt
1 1/2 teaspoons dried
  rosemary, crumbled
1 1/2 teaspoons dried thyme

ground black pepper
3 pounds boneless butterflied
  lamb leg, trimmed
1 tablespoon olive or vegetable oil
1/2 cup dry white wine
1/2 cup water

1. Preheat oven to 325°F. In 10-inch skillet, melt butter over medium heat. Add onion, garlic, 1 teaspoon salt, 3/4 teaspoon rosemary, 3/4 teaspoon thyme, and 1/4 teaspoon pepper and cook until onion is tender. Remove from heat.

2. Place lamb flat on work surface, cut side up; spread onion mixture evenly on lamb. Roll up lamb from one long side to enclose filling. Cut three 24-inch strings and one 34-inch string. Place long string horizontally on work surface, and short strings vertically across it. Set lamb, seam side up, lengthwise along long string. Tie strings around meat to secure.

3. Place lamb on rack in large roasting pan (17" by 11 1/2"). Rub with oil and remaining 3/4 teaspoon rosemary and remaining 3/4 teaspoon thyme; sprinkle with salt and pepper. Roast until meat thermometer inserted in center of lamb reaches 140°F, about 1 hour 45 minutes. Internal temperature of meat will rise to 145°F (medium) upon standing.

4. Transfer lamb to warm large platter; keep warm. Let stand 15 minutes to set juices for easier carving.

5. Add wine and water to roasting pan. Heat to boiling over high heat; stirring until browned bits are loosened from bottom of pan. Skim and discard fat.

6. Remove string from lamb; cut into thin slices. Serve lamb with gravy.

Each serving: About 250 calories, 29g protein, 2g carbohydrate, 13g total fat (5g saturated), 100mg cholesterol, 346mg sodium.

Herbed Lamb Rib Roast

When you feel like showing off a bit, few dishes do it more elegantly than a classic rack of lamb. For easier carving, ask the butcher to loosen the backbone from the ribs.

PREP: 10 MINUTES ROAST: 1 HOUR 5 MINUTES
MAKES 8 MAIN-DISH SERVINGS.

2 lamb rib roasts (racks of lamb),
   8 ribs each (2 1/2 pounds each),
   trimmed
1/2 teaspoon salt
3 tablespoons butter or margarine
2 cups fine fresh bread crumbs
   (about 4 slices firm white bread)

2 teaspoons dried rosemary,
   crumbled
1/4 teaspoon ground black pepper
2 tablespoons chopped fresh parsley
2 tablespoons Dijon mustard

1. Preheat oven to 375°F. In large roasting pan (17" by 11 1/2"), place roasts rib side down; sprinkle with salt. Roast lamb 50 minutes.

2. Meanwhile, in 10-inch skillet, melt butter over medium heat. Add bread crumbs, rosemary, and pepper and cook, stirring frequently, until crumbs are golden brown. Stir in parsley.

3. Spread mustard on tops of roasts. Press bread-crumb mixture onto mustard and pat so it adheres. Roast lamb until meat thermometer inserted in center of lamb (not touching bone) reaches 140°F, 15 to 20 minutes longer. Internal temperature of meat will rise to 145°F (medium) upon standing. Or roast to desired doneness.

4. When the roasts are done, transfer to cutting board and let stand for 10 minutes to set juices for easier carving. Cut off backbone from ribs. Transfer roasts to warm platter.

5. To serve, with sharp knife, cut lamb between bones to separate chops.

Each serving: About 311 calories, 27g protein, 7g carbohydrate, 18g total fat (8g saturated), 99mg cholesterol, 436mg sodium.

PORK & HAM

Pork Crown Roast with Apple Stuffing

Mustard-Glazed Fresh Ham with Cider Sauce

Cracklings, crunchy pieces of roasted pork skin, are a Southern treat. To try them, follow our directions in this recipe and cook them right along with the roast.

PREP: 20 MINUTES   ROAST: 5 HOURS   MAKES 24 MAIN-DISH SERVINGS.

1 whole pork leg (bone-in fresh ham) (15 pounds)
1 teaspoon Chinese five-spice powder (optional)
1/2 cup packed brown sugar
1 tablespoon dry mustard
1 tablespoon kosher salt
1 teaspoon coarsely ground pepper
1/4 teaspoon ground cloves
2 1/2 cups apple cider

1. Preheat oven to 350°F. With knife, remove skin from pork, if any, and reserve. Trim excess fat from pork; discard, leaving 1/4-inch-thick layer of fat. Place pork on rack in large roasting pan (17" by 11 1/2"). Insert meat thermometer into thickest part of pork, making sure thermometer is at least 1/2 inch from bone If you like, for cracklings, sprinkle reserved pork skin with five-spice powder. Place skin, fat side down, in 15 1/2" by 10 1/2" jelly-roll pan; set aside.

2. In small bowl, combine sugar, mustard, salt, pepper, and cloves. Rub sugar mixture on top and sides of pork, pressing lightly with hand so it adheres.

3. Roast pork and skin in same oven until thermometer registers 165°F and cracklings are browned and crisp (see Tip, page 141), 4 to 5 hours (16 to 20 minutes per pound). Internal temperature of pork will rise to 170°F upon standing. (Meat near bone may still be slightly pink.)

4. Transfer roast to warm large platter; let stand 20 minutes to set juices for easier carving. Remove cracklings from pan and drain on paper towels.

5. Remove rack from roasting pan. Strain pan drippings through sieve into medium bowl. Let stand until fat separates from pan juices, about 1 minute. Skim and discard fat. Return pan juices to hot roasting pan; add cider and heat to boiling over high heat, stirring until browned bits are loosened from bottom of pan. Boil until sauce thickens slightly, about 7 minutes. Strain sauce into gravy boat or serving bowl. Makes 2 3/4 cups.

6. Cut or break cracklings into serving-size pieces. Serve roast with cider sauce and cracklings, if you like.

Mustard-Glazed Fresh Ham with Cider Sauce

Each serving pork without cracklings or sauce: About 330 calories, 30g protein, 5g carbohydrate, 20g total fat (7g saturated), 107mg cholesterol, 255mg sodium.

Each ¼ cup cracklings: About 130 calories, 7g protein, 0g carbohydrate, 11g total fat (4g saturated), 19mg cholesterol, 365mg sodium.

Each tablespoon sauce: About 10 calories, 0g protein, 2g carbohydrate, 0g total fat, 0mg cholesterol, 45mg sodium.

TIP

Roasting time for fresh ham can vary by as much as an hour, depending on whether the meat contains a basting solution or was previously frozen and has not completely thawed internally (although it may appear thawed on the surface). The best way to make sure any meat is cooked to the proper temperature is to use a meat thermometer.

Fresh Ham with Two Sauces

This succulent fresh ham comes with a creamy mustard sauce as well as mushroom gravy to cover all the bases.

PREP: 30 MINUTES   ROAST: 5 HOURS 30 MINUTES
MAKES 30 MAIN-DISH SERVINGS.

1 whole pork leg (fresh ham)
  (15 pounds)
2 teaspoons dried sage
2 teaspoons salt
1 teaspoon ground black pepper

MUSTARD SAUCE
1 tablespoon vegetable oil
3 green onions, trimmed and
  thinly sliced

1/2 cup sour cream
1/3 cup Dijon mustard with seeds
1/3 cup milk

MUSHROOM PAN GRAVY
pan drippings from roasted fresh ham
1 pound mushrooms, trimmed
  and sliced
3 tablespoons all-purpose flour
chicken broth

1. Preheat oven to 325°F. Remove skin and trim excess fat from pork leg, leaving only a thin layer of fat. Score fat on top of pork leg in shallow parallel lines.

2. In cup, mix sage, salt, and pepper; use to rub on pork. Place pork, fat-side up, on rack in large roasting pan (17" by 11 1/2"). Roast pork until meat thermometer inserted into thickest part of pork (not touching bone) reaches 160°F, about 5 hours 30 minutes. If pork begins to brown too quickly, cover with loose tent of foil. Internal temperature of pork will rise to 170°F upon standing. (Meat near bone will be slightly pink.)

3. Meanwhile, prepare Mustard Sauce: In 2-quart saucepan, heat oil over medium-high heat; add green onions and cook until tender and lightly browned, about 5 minutes. Remove from heat. Stir in sour cream, mustard, and milk until blended. Cover and refrigerate until ready to serve.

4. When ham is done, transfer to large platter; keep warm. Let stand 30 minutes to set juices for easier carving.

5. Meanwhile, prepare Mushroom Pan Gravy: Remove rack from roasting pan. Strain pan drippings through sieve into 4-cup measuring cup; set roasting pan aside. Let stand until fat separates from pan juices, about 1 minute. Spoon 2 tablespoons fat into 12-inch skillet. Skim and discard the remaining fat.

6. Add the mushrooms to fat in skillet and cook over high heat until browned. Reduce heat to medium. Stir in flour; cook until lightly browned. Add enough chicken broth or *water* to juices in cup to equal 1 3/4 cups. Add about 1/2 cup pan-juice mixture to roasting pan; stirring until browned bits are loosened from bottom of pan. Add liquid from roasting pan and remaining pan-juice mixture to mushrooms; cook, stirring, over high heat until gravy boils and thickens. Makes about 3 cups.

7. To serve, cut ham into thin slices; serve with Mustard Sauce and Mushroom Pan Gravy.

Each serving: About 385 calories, 55g protein, 1g carbohydrate, 16g total fat (6g saturated), 131mg cholesterol, 360mg sodium.

Each 2 tablespoons gravy: About 20 calories, 1g protein, 2g carbohydrate, 1g total fat (0g saturated), 2mg cholesterol, 80mg sodium.

Slow-Roasted Fresh Ham

You can serve this savory dish with simple pan juices or your favorite piquant fruit chutney—either way it's mouthwatering.

PREP: 15 MINUTES   ROAST: 3 HOURS TO 3 HOURS 30 MINUTES
MAKES 12 MAIN-DISH SERVINGS.

3 tablespoons coriander seeds
2 tablespoons fennel seeds
2 teaspoons salt
4 garlic cloves, crushed with
  garlic press
1 tablespoon olive oil
2 teaspoons coarsely ground
  black pepper

1 shank or butt-half pork leg (fresh
  ham, 9 pounds)
1 can (14 1/2 ounces) reduced-sodium
  chicken broth
1/2 cup water

1. Preheat oven to 350°F. With knife, remove skin and trim excess fat from pork leg, leaving 1/4-inch layer of fat.

2. In mortar with pestle, crush coriander seeds and fennel seeds with salt (or, place seeds and salt in heavyweight ziptight plastic bag and crush seeds with rolling pin or heavy saucepan). In small bowl, combine seed mixture, garlic, oil, and pepper. Use to rub on pork. Place pork, fat side up, on rack in medium roasting pan (15 1/2" by 10 1/2"). Roast until meat thermometer inserted in thickest part of roast (not touching bone) reaches 160°F, about 3 hours. Internal temperature of meat will rise to 170°F upon standing. (Meat near bone will be slightly pink.)

3. When pork is done, transfer to warm large platter; keep warm. Let stand 15 minutes to set juices for easier carving.

4. Meanwhile, skim and discard fat from pan drippings. Add broth, water, and any meat juice from platter to roasting pan; heat to boiling over medium heat, stirring until browned bits from bottom of pan are loosened. Makes about 2 1/4 cups. Serve pan juices with pork.

Each serving: About 435 calories, 37g protein, 2g carbohydrate, 30g total fat (11g saturated), 132mg cholesterol, 475mg sodium.

Pork Roast with Fresh Sage

Our flavorful secret is a fresh-herb paste. For greater flavor absorption, rub the meat ahead of time and refrigerate for up to twenty-four hours. Bone-in cuts, such as this one, take a little longer to cook but are the most flavorful.

PREP: 15 MINUTES   ROAST: 2 HOURS TO 2 HOURS 15 MINUTES
MAKES 8 MAIN-DISH SERVINGS.

1/4 cup chopped fresh parsley	1/2 teaspoon ground black pepper
2 tablespoons chopped fresh sage	1 bone-in pork loin roast (4 pounds),
2 garlic cloves, finely chopped	trimmed
1/2 teaspoon dried thyme	1/3 cup dry white wine
1 teaspoon salt	2/3 cup chicken broth

1. Preheat oven to 350°F. On cutting board, chop parsley, sage, garlic, thyme, salt, and pepper together, occasionally crushing mixture with side of chef's knife, to make thick paste.

2. Place roast in small roasting pan (13" by 9") and rub herb paste on pork. Roast pork until meat thermometer inserted in thickest part of roast (not touching bone) reaches 160°F, 2 hours to 2 hours 15 minutes. Internal temperature of meat will rise to 170°F upon standing.

3. When roast is done, transfer to warm platter and let stand 15 minutes to set juices for easier carving.

4. Meanwhile, add wine to roasting pan and heat to boiling over high heat, stirring until browned bits are loosened from bottom of pan. Add broth and heat to boiling. Remove pan from heat; skim and discard fat. Serve sauce with roast.

Each serving: About 268 calories, 35g protein, 1g carbohydrate, 12g total fat (4g saturated), 99mg cholesterol, 440mg sodium.

Pork Crown Roast with Apple Stuffing

An elegant crown roast always makes a dramatic centerpiece for an important occasion. Be sure to order your roast ahead of time from your butcher. The savory apple stuffing is also good with roast turkey or goose.

PREP: 20 MINUTES   ROAST: 3 HOURS 30 MINUTES
MAKES 14 MAIN-DISH SERVINGS.

1 pork rib crown roast (7 pounds)
2 1/2 teaspoons salt
1/2 plus 1/8 teaspoon ground
  black pepper
6 tablespoons butter or margarine
4 stalks celery, chopped
1 large onion (12 ounces), chopped
1 pound Golden Delicious apples
  (3 medium), peeled, cored, and
  chopped

8 cups fresh bread cubes (10 to 12
  slices firm white bread)
1/2 cup apple juice
1 large egg, lightly beaten
1 teaspoon poultry seasoning
1/4 cup Calvados, applejack brandy,
  or water
3 tablespoons all-purpose flour
1 can (14 1/2 ounces) chicken broth

1. Preheat oven to 325°F. Rub roast with 1 teaspoon salt and 1/4 teaspoon pepper. Place roast, rib ends down, in large roasting pan (17" by 11 1/2"). Roast 1 hour.

2. Meanwhile, in 5-quart Dutch oven, melt butter over medium heat. Add the celery and onion and cook, stirring, until tender, about 5 minutes. Add apples and cook until tender, 6 to 8 minutes longer. Remove Dutch oven from heat. Stir in bread cubes, apple juice, egg, poultry seasoning, 1 teaspoon salt, and 1/4 teaspoon pepper. Toss until well combined.

3. Remove roast from oven and turn rib ends up. Fill cavity of roast with stuffing. (Place any leftover stuffing into greased 1 1/2-quart casserole. Bake leftover stuffing, uncovered, during last 30 minutes of roasting time.)

4. Return pork to oven and continue roasting until meat thermometer inserted in thickest part of roast (not touching bone) reaches 155°F, about 2 hours 30 minutes. Internal temperature of pork will rise to 160°F upon standing. If stuffing browns too quickly, cover it with foil.

5. When roast is done, transfer to warm platter and let stand 15 minutes to set juices for easier carving.

Pork Crown Roast with Apple Stuffing

6. Meanwhile, prepare gravy: Pour pan drippings into 2-cup measuring cup or medium bowl; let stand until fat separates from pan juices. Skim off 3 tablespoons fat from drippings; if necessary, add enough melted *butter* to equal 3 tablespoons. Pour into 2-quart saucepan. Skim and discard any remaining fat from pan juices. Add Calvados to roasting pan and heat over medium heat, stirring until browned bits are loosened from bottom of pan. Add to pan juices in measuring cup.

7. Into fat in saucepan, with wire whisk, whisk flour, remaining ½ teaspoon salt, and remaining ⅛ teaspoon pepper until blended; cook over medium heat 1 minute. Gradually whisk in pan-juice mixture and broth. Heat to boiling, stirring constantly; boil 1 minute. Serve roast warm with gravy and stuffing.

Each serving: About 406 calories, 32g protein, 19g carbohydrate, 21g total fat (9g saturated), 104mg cholesterol, 716mg sodium.

Pork Roast with Caraway Seeds

A simple but elegant roast loin of pork, dressed with an unusual crushed caraway seed, mustard, and herb coating. Serve with applesauce, if you like.

PREP: 10 MINUTES   ROAST: 2 HOURS 30 MINUTES
MAKES 10 MAIN-DISH SERVINGS.

2 tablespoons caraway seeds, crushed
1 teaspoon salt
1 teaspoon dry mustard
1/2 teaspoon dried thyme

1/2 teaspoon dried oregano
1 tablespoon vegetable oil
1 bone-in pork loin roast (6 pounds), trimmed
3 tablespoons all-purpose flour

1. Preheat oven to 325°F. In cup, combine caraway seeds, salt, dry mustard, thyme, oregano, and oil. Use to rub on fat side of roast.

2. Place roast, fat side up, on rack in large roasting pan (17" by 11 1/2"). Roast until meat thermometer inserted in thickest part of roast (not touching bone) reaches 155°F, about 2 hours 30 minutes. Internal temperature of meat will rise to 160°F upon standing.

3. When roast is done, transfer to warm platter and let stand 15 minutes to set juices for easier carving.

Each serving: About 334 calories, 43g protein, 3g carbohydrate, 16g total fat (5g saturated), 119mg cholesterol, 310mg sodium.

Garlic Roast Pork with Root Vegetables

Ask butcher to loosen backbone from ribs for easier slicing.

PREP: 10 MINUTES   ROAST: 1 HOUR 30 MINUTES
MAKES: 8 MAIN-DISH SERVINGS.

1 bone-in center-cut pork loin roast
  (4 pounds), trimmed
2 garlic cloves, cut into thin slivers
1 1/2 teaspoons salt
1/2 teaspoon coarsely ground pepper
2 small sweet potatoes (1 pound),
  peeled and cut into 2-inch chunks
1 medium fennel bulb (1 pound),
  trimmed and cut into 8 wedges

1 small rutabaga (1 1/4 pounds),
  peeled, halved, and cut into 1/2-
  inch-thick slices
2 parsnips (8 ounces), peeled and cut
  into 1-inch chunks
2 teaspoons olive oil
1 cup water

1. Preheat oven to 350°F. Cut about ten 1/2-inch-deep slits in pork and insert sliver of garlic in each. In cup, combine 1 teaspoon salt and 1/4 teaspoon pepper; use to rub on pork. Place pork, fat side up, in large roasting pan (17" by 11 1/2").

2. In large bowl, combine sweet potatoes, fennel, rutabaga, and parsnips. Sprinkle with oil, remaining 1/2 teaspoon salt and 1/4 teaspoon pepper; toss to coat. Arrange vegetables around pork in roasting pan.

3. Roast pork and vegetables until meat thermometer inserted in thickest part of roast (not touching bone) reaches 155°F, about 1 hour 30 minutes. Internal temperature of meat will rise on to 160°F upon standing.

4. When roast is done, transfer to warm large platter; with slotted spoon, transfer vegetables to same platter. Cover with foil and let roast stand 10 minutes to set juices for easier carving.

5. Meanwhile, add water to roasting pan; heat to boiling over medium-high heat, stirring until browned bits are loosened from bottom of pan. Remove pan from heat; skim and discard fat.

6. Remove and discard string, if any, from roast. Serve pork with vegetables and pan-juice mixture.

Each serving: About 420 calories, 37g protein, 23g carbohydrate, 19g total fat (7g saturated), 106mg cholesterol, 560mg sodium.

Roast Pork Loin with Apricot-Cranberry Pan Sauce

This succulent roast is served with a special "do-ahead" sauce made with dried fruits. A 5 1/2- to 6-pound roast should have ten ribs—check to make sure you have at least one per person.

PREP: 30 MINUTES PLUS STANDING   ROAST: 1 HOUR 30 MINUTES TO 2 HOURS
MAKES 10 MAIN-DISH SERVINGS.

PORK ROAST

1 pork loin roast (6 pounds), trimmed and backbone cracked

2 large lemons

2 garlic cloves, crushed with garlic press

1 tablespoon olive oil

2 teaspoons coarsely ground black pepper

1 teaspoon salt

APRICOT-CRANBERRY PAN SAUCE

2 tablespoons butter or margarine

1 small onion, finely chopped

1 can (14 1/2 ounces) chicken broth

1 cup dry Madeira wine

1/2 cup dried cranberries

1/2 cup dried apricots, chopped

1/2 cup loosely packed fresh parsley leaves, chopped

1. Preheat oven to 350°F. Pat pork loin dry with paper towels.

2. From lemons, grate 2 1/2 teaspoons peel and squeeze 1 tablespoon juice. In cup, mix lemon peel and juice, garlic, oil, pepper, and salt. Use to rub on pork.

3. Place pork on rack in medium roasting pan (15 1/2" by 10 1/2"). Roast pork until meat thermometer inserted in thickest part of roast (not touching bone) reaches 155°F, 1 1/2 to 2 hours. Internal temperature will rise to 160°F upon standing.

4. While pork is roasting, prepare fruit sauce: In 2-quart saucepan, melt butter over medium heat. Add onion and cook until tender and golden, about 10 minutes. Add broth, Madeira, cranberries, and apricots; heat to boiling over high heat. Boil, stirring occasionally, until sauce is reduced to about 2 2/3 cups, about 8 minutes. Remove saucepan from heat.

5. When pork is done, transfer to warm large platter; keep warm. Let stand 15 minutes to set juices for easier carving.

6. Meanwhile, skim fat from drippings in roasting pan and discard. Add fruit sauce to pan and cook over medium heat, stirring until browned bits are loosened from bottom of pan, about 1 minute. Stir in parsley.

7. To serve, add any meat juices from platter to sauce. Serve roast with Apricot-Cranberry Pan Sauce.

Each serving of roast: About 300 calories, 34g protein, 1g carbohydrate, 17g total fat (6g saturated), 77mg cholesterol, 300mg sodium.

Each ¼ cup Apricot-Cranberry Pan Sauce: About 70 calories, 2g protein, 10g carbohydrate, 3g total fat (1g saturated), 6mg cholesterol, 183mg sodium.

Roast Pork Loin with
Apricot-Cranberry Pan Sauce

Fennel-Rosemary Pork Roast

A sensational blend of spices is all it takes to make this tender roast taste great.

PREP: 20 MINUTES   ROAST: ABOUT 1 HOUR 30 MINUTES
MAKES 8 MAIN-DISH SERVINGS.

3 tablespoons rosemary leaves, chopped

2 tablespoons extravirgin olive oil

1 tablespoon fennel seeds, crushed

1½ teaspoons salt

1 teaspoon coarsely ground black pepper

7 garlic cloves, crushed with garlic press

1 bone-in pork loin roast (4 pounds), trimmed

⅓ cup water

1. Preheat oven to 350°F. In cup, combine rosemary, oil, fennel seeds, salt, pepper, and garlic to form a paste.

2. Place pork, fat side up, in small roasting pan (13" by 9"). Cut about twelve ½-inch-deep slits in pork. Fill each with some garlic mixture, reserving 2 tablespoons to rub on outside of pork.

3. Roast pork until meat thermometer inserted in thickest part of the pork (not touching bone) reaches 155°F, 1 hour 30 minutes to 1 hour 50 minutes. Internal temperature of meat will reach 160°F upon standing.

4. Transfer roast to warm platter; cover with foil and let stand 10 minutes to set juices for easier carving.

5. Meanwhile, skim and discard fat from drippings in pan. Add water to pan; heat to boiling over medium heat, stirring until browned bits are loosened from bottom of pan. Stir in any meat juices from platter.

6. Remove and discard string, if any, from roast. Serve pan-juice mixture with pork.

Each serving: About 305 calories, 30g protein, 2g carbohydrate, 19g total fat (6g saturated), 91mg cholesterol, 510mg sodium.

Caraway-Brined Pork Loin

Brining meat in an aromatic mixture of spices, sugar, and salt ensures succulence. For best flavor, allow pork to soak in brine up to twenty-four hours.

PREP: 20 MINUTES PLUS CHILLING AND MARINATING 18 TO 24 HOURS
ROAST: ABOUT 1 HOUR
MAKES 24 MAIN-DISH SERVINGS.

1/2 cup packed light brown sugar
1/2 cup kosher salt
1/4 cup caraway seeds, crushed
1/4 cup coriander seeds, cracked
3 tablespoons cracked black pepper
strips of peel from 2 lemons,
   pith removed

4 garlic cloves, crushed with side of
   chef's knife
2 boneless pork loin roasts (about
   3 pounds each)

1. In 1-quart saucepan, heat *1 cup water*, sugar, salt, caraway, coriander, pepper, and lemon peel to boiling over high heat. Reduce heat to low; simmer 2 minutes. Transfer mixture to large bowl; stir in garlic and *7 cups cold water*. Refrigerate 1 hour or freeze 30 minutes until brine is cool.

2. Place pork roasts in jumbo ziptight plastic bag with brine. Seal bag, pressing out excess air. Place bag in large bowl or roasting pan and refrigerate pork 18 to 24 hours.

3. When ready to cook pork, preheat oven to 400°F. Remove pork from bag; discard brine (it's OK if some seeds stick to pork). Place pork on rack in large roasting pan (17" by 11 1/2"). Roast pork until meat thermometer inserted in thickest part of pork reaches 155°F, about 1 hour to 1 hour and 15 minutes. Internal temperature of meat will reach 160°F upon standing. Transfer pork to cutting board and let stand 10 minutes to set juices for easier slicing.

4. Meanwhile, remove rack from roasting pan. Add *1/2 cup water* to pan and heat to boiling over medium-high heat, stirring until browned bits are loosened from bottom of pan, 2 minutes. Pour pan drippings through sieve into small bowl. Let stand until fat separates from pan juices; skim and discard fat. Spoon pan juices over sliced meat.

Each serving: About 205 calories, 22g protein, 1g carbohydrate, 12g total fat (4g saturated), 68mg cholesterol, 345mg sodium.

Caribbean Pork Roast

The seasonings that give this dish its Caribbean flavor are similar to those used in jerk cooking. The piquant sauce would also go well with grilled chicken or fish.

PREP: 10 MINUTES   ROAST: 1 HOUR 20 MINUTES
MAKES 6 MAIN-DISH SERVINGS.

1 boneless pork shoulder blade roast (fresh pork butt, 2 1/2 pounds), trimmed	1/2 teaspoon ground allspice
	1/2 teaspoon ground black pepper
	3 teaspoons Dijon mustard
1 1/2 teaspoons salt	2/3 cup mango chutney, chopped
1 1/4 teaspoons sugar	6 tablespoons fresh lime juice
3/4 teaspoon ground ginger	2 tablespoons water

1. Preheat oven to 425°F. Using sharp knife, cut roast lengthwise almost in half, being careful not to cut all the way through. Open and spread flat like a book. In cup, combine salt, sugar, ginger, allspice, and pepper. Brush cut side of pork with 2 teaspoons mustard and sprinkle with half of seasoning mixture. Close pork "book" and rub remaining seasoning mixture on outside of pork. Tie roast with string at 1-inch intervals. Place roast on rack in small roasting pan (13" by 9").

2. Roast pork 1 hour. Turn oven control to 350°F and roast until meat thermometer inserted in center of roast reaches 155°F, about 20 minutes longer. Internal temperature of meat will rise to 160°F upon standing.

3. Transfer pork to platter; keep warm. Let stand 10 minutes to set juices for easier slicing.

4. Meanwhile, in small bowl, combine chutney, lime juice, water, and the remaining 1 teaspoon mustard. Serve sauce with sliced pork.

Each serving: About 417 calories, 35g protein, 28g carbohydrate, 17g total fat (6g saturated), 124mg cholesterol, 1,050mg sodium.

Caribbean Pork Roast

French Roast Pork

The spice mixture rubbed onto the pork is a classic French combination known as *quatre épices*, which means "four spices." We've taken the liberty of adding a few more spices for good measure. Once the pork begins roasting, the scent of warm spices will fill your kitchen.

PREP: 5 MINUTES ROAST: 1 HOUR MAKES 6 MAIN-DISH SERVINGS.

**1 boneless pork loin roast
  (2 pounds), trimmed**
1 teaspoon salt
3/4 teaspoon dried thyme
1/2 teaspoon ground cinnamon
1/2 teaspoon ground black pepper

1/8 teaspoon ground nutmeg
1/8 teaspoon ground cloves
1/3 cup dry white wine
2/3 cup chicken broth
applesauce

1. Preheat oven to 350°F. Pat pork dry with paper towels.

2. In cup, combine salt, thyme, cinnamon, pepper, nutmeg, and cloves. Use to rub on pork.

3. Place roast on rack in small roasting pan (13" by 9"). Roast pork until meat thermometer inserted in center of roast reaches 155°F, about 1 hour. Internal temperature of meat will rise to 160°F upon standing.

4. When roast is done, transfer to warm platter and let stand 15 minutes to set juices for easier slicing.

5. Meanwhile, add wine to roasting pan and heat to boiling over high heat, stirring until browned bits are loosened from bottom of pan. Add broth and heat to boiling; boil 2 minutes. Remove pan from heat; skim and discard fat. Serve pan juices and applesauce with pork.

Each serving: About 254 calories, 33g protein, 1g carbohydrate, 11g total fat (4g saturated), 93mg cholesterol, 561mg sodium.

Orange Roast Pork with Cumin

We used cumin and cayenne pepper to add a little pizzazz to this succulent roast, then whipped up an easy pan sauce to spoon over the tender slices.

PREP: 15 MINUTES PLUS STANDING   ROAST: 1 HOUR 15 MINUTES
MAKES 6 MAIN-DISH SERVINGS.

1 boneless pork loin roast
   (2 pounds), trimmed
1 garlic clove, minced
2 teaspoons grated orange peel
1 teaspoon salt
3/4 teaspoon ground cumin
1/2 teaspoon dried oregano

1/2 teaspoon dried thyme
1/4 teaspoon ground red pepper
   (cayenne)
1 medium onion, finely chopped
2 tablespoons cider vinegar
3/4 cup chicken broth

1. Preheat oven to 350°F. Pat pork dry with paper towels. With small knife, cut several 1/2-inch-deep slits in pork.

2. In cup, mix garlic, orange peel, salt, cumin, oregano, thyme, and ground red pepper. Use to rub over pork, pressing into crevices and slits.

3. Spread chopped onion in small roasting pan (11" by 7"); place pork roast on top. Roast pork until meat thermometer inserted in thickest part of pork reaches 155°F, about 1 hour 15 minutes. Internal temperature of meat will rise to 160°F upon standing.

4. Transfer pork to platter; keep warm. Let stand 5 minutes to set juices for easier slicing.

5. Skim and discard fat from drippings in roasting pan. Add vinegar to pan and heat to boiling over high heat, stirring until browned bits are loosened from bottom of pan. Boil 1 minute. Add broth to pan and heat to boiling; boil 3 minutes. Serve pan juices with sliced pork.

Each serving: About 240 calories, 25mg protein, 4g carbohydrate, 13g total fat (5g saturated), 76mg cholesterol, 535mg sodium.

Oven-Barbecued Spareribs

These sweet and sticky ribs are worth getting your fingers dirty for!

PREP: 10 MINUTES   ROAST: 1 HOUR 30 MINUTES
MAKES 6 MAIN-DISH SERVINGS.

6 pounds pork spareribs, cut into
  1-rib portions
1 can (6 ounces) tomato paste
1/4 cup packed brown sugar
1/2 cup water
1/4 cup honey

1/4 cup cider vinegar
2 tablespoons vegetable oil
1 tablespoon grated onion
2 teaspoons chili powder
2 teaspoons salt

1. Preheat oven to 325°F. Arrange spareribs in single layer in large roasting pan (17" by 11 1/2"). Roast spareribs 1 hour.

2. Meanwhile, prepare glaze: In medium bowl, combine tomato paste, brown sugar, water, honey, vinegar, oil, onion, chili powder, and salt until well blended.

3. Brush ribs with glaze. Roast ribs, brushing frequently with glaze, until ribs are tender, about 30 minutes longer.

Each serving: About 849 calories, 53g protein, 27g carbohydrate, 59g total fat (20g saturated), 214mg cholesterol, 1,178mg sodium.

Mexican-Style Spareribs

A heady blend of tequila, orange juice, lime juice, and jalapeño pepper gives these pork ribs their personality. If you wish, the ribs can be marinated for as long as overnight.

PREP: 15 MINUTES   ROAST: 1 HOUR 50 MINUTES
MAKES 4 MAIN-DISH SERVINGS.

1 cup firmly packed fresh cilantro
    leaves and stems
1/2 small onion, thinly sliced
4 garlic cloves, crushed with
    garlic press
1 pickled jalapeño chile
1/2 cup fresh lime juice

1/4 cup fresh orange juice
1/4 cup tequila
1 tablespoon olive oil
2 tablespoons sugar
1/2 teaspoon dried oregano
3 pounds pork spareribs

1. Preheat oven to 350°F. In blender, combine cilantro, onion, garlic, pickled jalapeño, lime and orange juices, tequila, oil, sugar, and oregano and puree until smooth.

2. Place spareribs in nonreactive roasting pan just large enough to hold them in single layer. Pour cilantro mixture over ribs, turning until evenly coated. Roast, turning ribs twice, 1 hour 30 minutes. Turn oven control to 450°F and roast the ribs until very tender and richly colored, about 20 minutes longer.

3. Transfer ribs to warm platter. Skim and discard fat from sauce remaining in pan and spoon sauce over ribs.

Each serving: About 610 calories, 40g protein, 13g carbohydrate, 44g total fat (15g saturated), 161mg cholesterol, 183mg sodium.

Pork Tenderloin with Dijon-Fennel Rub and Sweet-Potato Fries

Pork Tenderloin with Dijon-Fennel Rub & Sweet-Potato Fries

An easy rub seasons this lean and tender cut of pork. Cook fries in the same oven while the pork roasts.

PREP: 15 MINUTES   ROAST: 25 MINUTES   MAKES: 4 MAIN-DISH SERVINGS.

SWEET-POTATO FRIES
nonstick cooking spray
2 medium sweet potatoes
   (about 1¼ pounds)
½ teaspoon salt

DIJON-FENNEL PORK
1 tablespoon Dijon mustard
2 teaspoons fennel seeds, crushed

1 garlic clove, crushed with garlic
   press
½ teaspoon dried thyme
½ teaspoon salt
½ teaspoon ground black pepper
1 whole pork tenderloin (1 pound)

1. Prepare fries: Preheat oven to 475°F. Spray 15½" by 10½" jelly-roll pan or large cookie sheet with nonstick cooking spray.

2. Scrub potatoes well but do not peel. Slice each potato lengthwise in half. Holding each potato half cut side down, cut lengthwise into ¼-inch-thick slices. Arrange potatoes in single layer in prepared jelly-roll pan; sprinkle with salt and lightly coat with nonstick cooking spray.

3. Prepare pork: In small bowl, mix mustard, fennel seeds, garlic, thyme, salt, and pepper. Use to rub on pork. Place pork on rack in small roasting pan (14" by 10"). Turn thin ends of pork under for even thickness.

4. Roast potatoes and pork on 2 oven racks until meat thermometer inserted in center of pork reaches 155°F and potatoes are tender and lightly browned, about 25 minutes. Internal temperature of pork will rise to 160°F upon standing.

5. Transfer pork to cutting board. Let stand 5 minutes to set juices for easier slicing. Transfer potatoes to serving bowl. With knife held in slanting position, almost parallel to cutting board, cut tenderloin into ¼-inch-thick slices. Serve pork with potatoes.

Each serving: About 300 calories, 27g protein, 36g carbohydrate, 5g total fat (2g saturated), 67mg cholesterol, 670mg sodium.

Sesame Pork Tenderloins

Whole pork tenderloins are brushed with a flavorful mixture of hoisin sauce, ginger, and sesame oil, then coated with sesame seeds and roasted until golden. Just slice and serve over rice, or serve the sliced pork "Peking duck–style," tucked into warm flour tortillas with green onion and cucumber.

PREP: 15 MINUTES   ROAST: 30 MINUTES   MAKES 6 MAIN-DISH SERVINGS.

1/4 cup hoisin sauce
1 tablespoon grated, peeled
   fresh ginger
1/2 teaspoon Asian sesame oil

1/3 cup sesame seeds
2 whole pork tenderloins
   (12 ounces each)

1. Preheat oven to 475°F. In small bowl, whisk hoisin sauce, ginger, and sesame oil until blended.

2. Spread sesame seeds in even layer on waxed paper. With pastry brush, spread hoisin mixture on tenderloins, then roll pork in sesame seeds until evenly coated.

3. Place tenderloins on rack in small roasting pan (13" by 9"). Turn thin ends of pork under for even thickness. Roast 15 minutes; turn tenderloins over and roast until thermometer inserted in center of each pork tenderloin reaches 155°F, about 15 minutes longer. Internal temperature will rise to 160°F upon standing.

4. Transfer tenderloins to cutting board. Let stand 5 minutes to set juices for easier slicing.

Each serving: About 215 calories, 26g protein, 7g carbohydrate, 9g total fat (2g saturated), 68mg cholesterol, 220mg sodium.

Jamaican Roast Pork Tenderloins

We used both sweet and hot spices plus a dash of rum to make this fabulous roast. Serve it with oven roasted potatoes, or rice, black beans, and sautéed bananas.

Prep: 10 minutes Roast: 30 to 35 minutes
Makes 6 main-dish servings.

2 pork tenderloins (12 ounces each)
1 garlic clove, minced
1 tablespoon brown sugar
1 teaspoon grated lime peel
1/2 teaspoon ground ginger
1/2 teaspoon salt
1/4 teaspoon ground black pepper

1/8 teaspoon ground nutmeg
1/8 teaspoon ground allspice
1/8 teaspoon ground red pepper (cayenne)
2 teaspoons plus 2 tablespoons dark rum
1 1/4 cups chicken broth

1. Preheat oven to 450°F. Pat pork dry with paper towels. Place pork in small roasting pan (13" by 9"). Turn thin ends of the pork under for even thickness.

2. In cup, mix garlic, brown sugar, lime peel, ginger, salt, black pepper, nutmeg, allspice, ground red pepper, and 2 teaspoons rum. Use to rub on tenderloins. Pour 1/4 cup broth into pan around pork.

3. Roast pork until meat thermometer inserted in center of each tenderloin reaches 155°F, 30 to 35 minutes, adding 1/4 cup more broth to roasting pan after 10 minutes and another 1/4 cup after 20 minutes to prevent pan juices from burning. Internal temperature of meat will rise to 160°F upon standing.

4. Transfer pork to platter; keep warm. Let stand 10 minutes to set juices for easier slicing.

5. Add remaining 2 tablespoons rum to roasting pan and heat to boiling over high heat, stirring until browned bits are loosened from bottom of pan; boil 1 minute. Add remaining 1/2 cup broth to pan; heat to boiling. Slice pork thin and serve with pan juices.

Each serving: About 170 calories, 24g protein, 3g carbohydrate, 5g total fat (2g saturated), 70mg cholesterol, 445mg sodium.

FISH & SHELLFISH

Halibut with Baby Artichokes & Potatoes

Tarragon-Roasted Salmon

No fish poacher? Roast a whole salmon in the oven!

PREP: 10 MINUTES   ROAST: 40 MINUTES   MAKES 10 MAIN-DISH SERVINGS.

2 large lemons, thinly sliced
1 whole salmon (5 1/2 pounds),
cleaned and scaled
2 tablespoons olive oil
1/2 teaspoon salt
1/2 teaspoon coarsely ground
black pepper

1 large bunch tarragon
1 small bunch parsley
Caper Sauce (below)
lemon wedges

1. Preheat oven to 450°F. Line jelly-roll pan (15 1/2" by 10 1/2") with foil.
2. Place one-third of lemon slices in row down center of pan. Rinse salmon inside and out with cold running water; pat dry with paper towels. Rub outside of salmon with oil. Place salmon on top of lemon slices. Sprinkle cavity with salt and pepper. Place tarragon and parsley sprigs and half of remaining lemon slices in cavity. Arrange remaining lemon slices on top of fish.
3. Roast salmon until just opaque throughout when knife is inserted at backbone, about 40 minutes.
4. Meanwhile, prepare Caper Sauce.
5. Carefully remove lemon slices and peel off skin from top of salmon; discard. Using two wide spatulas, transfer salmon to cutting board.
6. To serve, slide metal spatula under front section of top fillet and lift off fillet; transfer to warm large platter. Lift backbone away from bottom fillet; discard backbone. Slide spatula between bottom fillet and skin and transfer fillet to platter. Serve with lemon wedges and the caper sauce.

Each serving without sauce: About 325 calories, 33g protein, 1g carbohydrate, 20g total fat (4g saturated), 96mg cholesterol, 213mg sodium.

Caper Sauce

In medium bowl, mix **³/₄ cup sour cream**, **¹/₂ cup mayonnaise**, **¹/₄ cup milk**, **3 tablespoons capers**, drained and chopped, **2 tablespoons chopped fresh tarragon**, **¹/₂ teaspoon freshly grated lemon peel**, and **¹/₈ teaspoon coarsely ground black pepper** until blended. Cover and refrigerate until ready to serve, up to 2 days. Makes about 1²/₃ cups.

Each tablespoon: About 58 calories, 0g protein, 1g carbohydrate, 6g total fat (2g saturated), 7mg cholesterol, 90mg sodium.

**Slide metal spatula under front section of top fillet;
lift off and transfer to platter.**

**Lift backbone away from bottom fillet; discard backbone.
Slide spatula between bottom fillet and skin; transfer fillet to platter.**

Roasted Striped Bass with Salsa Verde

Serve this dramatic-looking entrée with Salsa Verde or, if time is limited, with lemon wedges.

PREP: 5 MINUTES   ROAST: 30 MINUTES   MAKES 4 MAIN-DISH SERVINGS.

1 whole striped bass (2¼ pounds), cleaned and scaled
3 thin slices lemon

3 rosemary sprigs (optional)
Salsa Verde (page 169)

1. Preheat oven to 450°F. Rinse bass inside and out with cold running water; pat dry with paper towels. Place lemon slices and rosemary, if using, in cavity. Make diagonal slashes on each side of fish at 1-inch intervals, about ¼ inch deep. Place bass in medium roasting pan (14" by 10").

2. Roast bass until just opaque throughout when knife is inserted at backbone, about 30 minutes.

3. Meanwhile, prepare Salsa Verde.

4. Carefully remove lemon slices and rosemary and peel off skin from top of bass; discard. Using two wide spatulas, transfer bass to cutting board.

5. To serve, slide cake server under front section of top fillet and lift off fillet; transfer to platter. Slide server under backbone and lift it away from bottom fillet; discard. Slide cake server between bottom fillet and skin and transfer fillet to platter.

Each serving: About 117 calories, 20g protein, 0g carbohydrate, 4g total fat (1g saturated), 88mg cholesterol, 76mg sodium.

Salsa Verde (Green Sauce)

With the side of chef's knife, mash **1 large clove garlic**, minced, and **1/4 teaspoon salt** to a smooth paste. In blender or in food processor with knife blade attached, puree **2 cups tightly packed fresh parsley leaves**, **8 anchovy fillets**, drained and chopped, if you like, the garlic paste, **1 teaspoon Dijon mustard**, **1/8 teaspoon ground black pepper**, **1/2 cup olive oil**, and **3 tablespoons fresh lemon juice** until very smooth. If not serving right away, cover and refrigerate up to 4 hours. Makes about 1 cup.

Each tablespoon: About 73 calories, 1g protein, 2g carbohydrate, 7g total fat (1g saturated), 1mg cholesterol, 125mg sodium.

Halibut with Baby Artichokes & Potatoes

Fish, potatoes, and artichokes are tossed in a lemon-and-oregano blend, then roasted together in one pan.

PREP: 20 MINUTES   ROAST: 40 MINUTES   MAKES: 4 MAIN-DISH SERVINGS.

2 lemons, 1 cut in half
3 tablespoons olive oil
1 teaspoon salt
1 teaspoon dried oregano
1/2 teaspoon coarsely ground
   black pepper
1 1/2 pounds small red potatoes, cut
   into 1-inch chunks

1 jumbo onion (1 pound),
   cut into 8 wedges
12 baby artichokes (1 1/2 pounds)
4 halibut or cod steaks, 1 inch thick
   (6 ounces each)
lemon wedges

1. Preheat oven to 450°F. From whole lemon, grate 1 tablespoon peel and squeeze 1 tablespoon juice. In small bowl, combine lemon peel and juice with oil, salt, oregano, and pepper. In large bowl, toss potatoes and onion with 1 tablespoon lemon mixture to coat well. Place potato mixture in 15 1/2" by 10 1/2" jelly-roll pan and roast 25 minutes.

2. Meanwhile, trim baby artichokes: Bend back outer green leaves and snap off at base until remaining leaves are green on top and yellow on bottom. Cut off stems level with bottom of artichoke. Cut off top half of each artichoke and discard. Cut each artichoke lengthwise in half. Rub cut surfaces with lemon halves to prevent discoloration.

3. In 3-quart saucepan, heat *4 cups water* to boiling over high heat. Add artichokes and cook until fork-tender, 6 to 8 minutes; drain. Toss artichokes with 2 tablespoons lemon mixture.

4. Remove pan with potato mixture from oven; add artichokes and toss well. Arrange fish on top of vegetables; brush with remaining lemon mixture. Return pan to oven and roast until fish turns opaque throughout and potatoes are fork-tender and lightly browned, about 15 minutes longer.

5. Transfer fish and vegetables to platter. Serve with lemon wedges.

Each serving: About 495 calories, 42g protein, 50g carbohydrate, 15g total fat (2g saturated), 54mg cholesterol, 735mg sodium.

Halibut with Baby
Artichokes & Potatoes

Soy-Glazed Salmon with Spinach

Salmon steaks are roasted with a flavorful Asian glaze, with no added fat. Prewashed, bagged baby spinach leaves need no cooking—the heat of the salmon served on top wilts them perfectly.

PREP: 15 MINUTES   ROAST: 10 MINUTES
MAKES 4 MAIN-DISH SERVINGS.

4 salmon steaks (6 ounces each)
1/4 cup reduced-sodium soy sauce
2 tablespoons seasoned rice vinegar
1 garlic clove, crushed with
   garlic press
1 tablespoon grated, peeled
   fresh ginger

1 tablespoon dark brown sugar
2 teaspoons cornstarch
1/8 teaspoon crushed red pepper
2 tablespoons water
1 bag (6 ounces) baby spinach

1. Preheat oven to 450°F. Arrange salmon steaks in small greased glass baking dish (13" by 9"). Roast 5 minutes.

2. Meanwhile, in small bowl, whisk soy sauce, vinegar, garlic, ginger, sugar, cornstarch, crushed red pepper, and water until blended. Pour glaze over salmon. Roast salmon until just opaque throughout and glaze has thickened, about 5 minutes longer.

3. To serve, divide spinach among 4 plates. Top spinach with salmon and drizzle with remaining glaze.

Each serving: About 280 calories, 33g protein, 10g carbohydrate, 11g total fat (3g saturated), 72mg cholesterol, 895mg sodium.

Roasted Scrod with Tomato Relish

A sweet-and-sour relish is just the thing to perk up scrod fillets.

PREP: 15 MINUTES   COOK/ROAST: 40 MINUTES
MAKES 4 MAIN-DISH SERVINGS.

1 can (28 ounces) plum tomatoes	2 tablespoons brown sugar
3 teaspoons vegetable oil	1/2 teaspoon salt
1 small onion, chopped	4 pieces scrod fillet (6 ounces each)
2 tablespoons water	1/4 teaspoon coarsely ground
1/4 cup red wine vinegar	black pepper

1. Preheat oven to 450°F. Drain tomatoes; cut each tomato into quarters.

2. In 2-quart saucepan, heat 2 teaspoons oil over medium heat. Add onion and water and cook until tender and golden, about 10 minutes. Stir in tomatoes, vinegar, brown sugar, and 1/4 teaspoon salt; heat to boiling over high heat. Continue cooking over high heat, stirring frequently, until relish has thickened, about 15 minutes.

3. Meanwhile, with tweezers, remove any bones from scrod. Arrange fillets in 9-inch square baking dish; sprinkle with remaining 1 teaspoon oil, pepper, and remaining 1/4 teaspoon salt. Roast scrod until just opaque throughout, 12 to 15 minutes.

4. To serve, transfer fish to plates and spoon tomato relish on top.

Each serving: About 248 calories, 32g protein, 18g carbohydrate, 5g total fat (1g saturated), 73mg cholesterol, 708mg sodium.

Roast Salmon with Capers & Parsley

Roast Salmon with Capers & Parsley

A whole salmon fillet with a crusty crumb-and-herb topping looks festive, tastes fabulous, and is surprisingly quick and easy to prepare.

PREP: 10 MINUTES   ROAST: 30 MINUTES
MAKES 6 MAIN-DISH SERVINGS.

3 tablespoons butter or margarine
1/3 cup plain dried bread crumbs
1/4 cup loosely packed fresh parsley
  leaves, minced
3 tablespoons drained capers,
  minced
1 teaspoon dried tarragon, crumbled
2 teaspoons grated fresh
  lemon peel

1/4 teaspoon salt
1/4 teaspoon coarsely ground
  black pepper
1 whole salmon fillet (about
  2 pounds)
lemon wedges

1. Preheat oven to 450°F. In 1-quart saucepan, melt butter over low heat. Remove saucepan from heat; stir in bread crumbs, parsley, capers, tarragon, lemon peel, salt, and pepper.

2. Line 15 1/2" by 10 1/2" jelly-roll pan with foil; grease foil. Place salmon, skin side down, in pan and pat crumb mixture on top. Roast until salmon turns opaque throughout and the topping is lightly browned, about 30 minutes.

3. With 2 large spatulas, carefully transfer salmon to platter. (It's okay if salmon skin sticks to foil.) Serve with lemon wedges.

Each serving: About 325 calories, 28g protein, 5g carbohydrate, 21g total fat (7g saturated), 94mg cholesterol, 407mg sodium.

Maple-Glazed Salmon

This pungent glaze is packed with sweet and tangy flavors. We love it combined with the richness of salmon, but it would taste equally good on swordfish or scrod.

PREP: 10 MINUTES   ROAST: 15 MINUTES
MAKES 4 MAIN-DISH SERVINGS.

3 tablespoons pure maple syrup
2 tablespoons soy sauce
1 tablespoon grated, peeled
   fresh ginger

1/2 teaspoon cornstarch
1 tablespoon water
4 salmon fillets (6 ounces each)
1 green onion, thinly sliced

1. Preheat oven to 475°F. In small bowl, with wire whisk or fork, mix maple syrup, soy sauce, ginger, cornstarch, and water until blended.
2. In shallow 1 1/2-quart casserole, arrange salmon, skin side down. Spoon glaze over fish and roast, without turning, until just opaque throughout, about 15 minutes, basting once halfway through cooking time. To serve, sprinkle with green onion.

Each serving: About 340 calories, 32g protein, 12g carbohydrate, 18g total fat (4g saturated), 89mg cholesterol, 580mg sodium.

Roasted Salmon & Dilled Potatoes

Using one pan to oven-roast the potatoes and the fish means preparation and cleanup are a breeze.

PREP: 15 MINUTES   ROAST: 25 MINUTES
MAKES 4 MAIN-DISH SERVINGS.

1 1/2 pounds red potatoes, cut into
  1-inch chunks
1 tablespoon olive oil
3/4 teaspoon salt
1/8 teaspoon coarsely ground
  black pepper

4 salmon fillets (6 ounces each)
2 tablespoons prepared
  horseradish sauce
1/2 cup loosely packed fresh dill,
  chopped

1. Preheat oven to 450°F. In 15 1/2" by 10 1/2" jelly-roll pan, toss potatoes with oil, 1/4 teaspoon salt, and 1/8 teaspoon pepper. Roast potatoes for 10 minutes.

2. Remove potatoes from oven. With spatula, push potatoes to one end of pan. Arrange fish in pan; sprinkle with remaining 1/2 teaspoon salt. Roast until fish is just opaque throughout and potatoes are browned and tender, about 15 minutes.

3. Transfer fish to platter and top with horseradish sauce; sprinkle with half of dill. Toss potatoes with remaining dill; arrange on platter with fish.

Each serving: About 495 calories, 35g protein, 38g carbohydrate, 23g total fat (5g saturated), 92mg cholesterol, 555mg sodium.

VEGETABLES

Oven-Browned Carrots
& Parsnips

Roasted Asparagus

This method, which intensifies the flavor of asparagus, could easily become your favorite preparation.

PREP: 12 MINUTES   ROAST: 20 MINUTES
MAKES 6 ACCOMPANIMENT SERVINGS.

2 pounds asparagus, trimmed
1 tablespoon olive oil
1/2 teaspoon salt
1/4 teaspoon coarsely ground
   black pepper

freshly grated lemon peel (optional)
lemon wedges

1. Preheat oven to 450°F.

2. In large roasting pan (17" by 11 1/2"), toss asparagus, oil, salt, and pepper until coated.

3. Roast asparagus, shaking pan occasionally, until tender and lightly browned, about 20 minutes. Sprinkle with grated lemon peel, if you like, and serve with lemon wedges.

Each serving: About 47 calories, 4g protein, 5g carbohydrate, 3g total fat (0g saturated), 0mg cholesterol, 195mg sodium.

Roasted Green Beans in Dill Vinaigrette

Simple to make and equally roasted green beans good served warm or at room temperature.

PREP: 20 MINUTES   ROAST: 20 TO 30 MINUTES
MAKES 8 ACCOMPANIMENT SERVINGS.

2 pounds green beans, trimmed
3 tablespoons olive oil
3/4 teaspoon salt
2 tablespoons white wine vinegar
11/2 teaspoons Dijon mustard

1/2 teaspoon sugar
1/2 teaspoon coarsely ground
    black pepper
2 tablespoons chopped fresh dill

1. Preheat oven to 450°F. In large roasting pan (17" by 11 1/2"), toss green beans with 1 tablespoon olive oil and 1/2 teaspoon salt. Roast beans, stirring twice, until tender and slightly browned, 20 to 30 minutes.

2. Meanwhile, prepare vinaigrette: In small bowl, with wire whisk, mix vinegar, mustard, sugar, the remaining 1/4 teaspoon salt, and pepper until blended. In thin, steady stream, whisk in remaining 2 tablespoons oil until blended; stir in dill.

3. When green beans are done, transfer to serving bowl. Drizzle vinaigrette over green beans; toss until evenly coated.

Each serving: About 80 calories, 2g protein, 8g carbohydrate, 5g total fat (1g saturated), 0mg cholesterol, 230mg sodium.

Roasted Green Beans with Mint & Oregano

You'll love the flavor of these green beans. They're oven-roasted, then tossed with a lemony vinaigrette. Serve warm or at room temperature.

PREP: 20 MINUTES   ROAST: 25 MINUTES
MAKES 8 ACCOMPANIMENT SERVINGS.

2 1/2 pounds green beans, trimmed
3 tablespoons olive oil
3/4 teaspoon salt
2 lemons
1/4 teaspoon coarsely ground
  black pepper

1/2 cup loosely packed fresh mint
  leaves, chopped
2 tablespoons loosely packed fresh
  oregano leaves, chopped

1. Preheat oven to 450°F. In large roasting pan (17" by 11 1/2"), toss green beans with 1 tablespoon oil and 1/2 teaspoon salt. Roast beans, stirring twice, until tender and slightly browned, 25 to 30 minutes.

2. Meanwhile, from the lemons, grate 1 tablespoon peel and squeeze 2 tablespoons juice. In large bowl, with wire whisk, mix lemon peel and juice, black pepper, remaining 2 tablespoons olive oil, and the remaining 1/4 teaspoon salt until blended.

3. When green beans are done, add to vinaigrette in bowl. Add mint and oregano; toss until beans are evenly coated. Serve warm or cover and refrigerate up to one day.

Each serving: About 90 calories, 3g protein, 10g carbohydrate, 5g total fat (1g saturated), 0mg cholesterol, 225mg sodium.

Roasted Beets & Onions

Roasted beets have a deep purple color and virtually burst with sweetness. The balsamic vinegar sauce enhances their naturally rich flavor.

PREP: 20 MINUTES PLUS COOLING   ROAST/COOK: 1 HOUR 40 MINUTES
MAKES 6 ACCOMPANIMENT SERVINGS.

2 bunches beets with tops (2 pounds)	1 teaspoon brown sugar
3 small red onions (1 pound), not peeled	1 teaspoon fresh thyme
	1/4 teaspoon salt
2 tablespoons extravirgin olive oil	1/4 teaspoon coarsely ground black pepper
1/3 cup chicken broth	1 tablespoon chopped fresh parsley
1/4 cup balsamic vinegar	

1. Preheat oven to 400°F.

2. Trim all but 1 inch of stems from beets. Place beets and onions in non-stick oven-safe 10-inch skillet (if skillet is not oven-safe, wrap handle with double layer of foil) or in 13" by 9" baking pan; drizzle with oil. Roast, shaking skillet occasionally, until onions have softened and beets are tender, about 1 hour 30 minutes, transferring the vegetables to plate as they are done.

3. In same skillet, combine broth, vinegar, brown sugar, and thyme; heat to boiling over high heat. Boil, stirring and scraping bottom of skillet, until vinegar mixture is dark brown and syrupy and has reduced to about 1/4 cup, 5 to 7 minutes; stir in salt and pepper. Remove from heat.

4. When cool enough to handle, peel beets and onions. Cut the beets into 1/4-inch-wide matchstick strips and onions into thin rounds; place in bowl. Pour vinegar mixture over vegetables and toss until coated. Sprinkle with parsley.

Each serving: About 103 calories, 2g protein, 14g carbohydrate, 5g total fat (1g saturated), 0mg cholesterol, 203mg sodium.

Broccoli with Thai Peanut Sauce

Roast broccoli flowerets and stems, then toss with our delectable sauce and top with chopped peanuts. Asian fish sauce is available in specialty sections of some supermarkets and in Asian grocery stores.

PREP: 20 MINUTES   ROAST: 25 MINUTES
MAKES 6 ACCOMPANIMENT SERVINGS.

1 large bunch broccoli (about
   1³/₄ pounds), flowerets cut into
   bite-size pieces and stems peeled
   and cut into ¹/₄-inch-thick slices
1 tablespoon vegetable oil
1 tablespoon minced, peeled
   fresh ginger
1 garlic clove, crushed with
   garlic press

2 teaspoons Asian fish sauce
   (nuoc nam)
2 tablespoons fresh lime juice
1 tablespoon sugar
³/₄ cup loosely packed fresh cilantro
   leaves, chopped
2 tablespoons unsalted roasted
   peanuts, coarsely chopped

1. Preheat oven to 450°F. In two 15¹/₂" by 10¹/₂" jelly-roll pans, toss broccoli with oil until evenly coated. Roast broccoli, until tender and lightly browned, 20 minutes, stirring occasionally and rotating pans between upper and lower racks halfway through roasting time. Stir in ginger and garlic; roast 3 to 5 minutes longer.

2. In large bowl, mix fish sauce, lime juice, and sugar. Add broccoli and cilantro; toss to coat. To serve, sprinkle with peanuts.

Each serving: About 90 calories, 6g protein, 11g carbohydrate, 4g total fat (1g saturated), 0mg cholesterol, 190mg sodium.

Roasted Cauliflower

Cauliflower becomes lightly browned and tender-crisp when roasted. It's a delicious change from the familiar boiled version.

PREP: 10 MINUTES   ROAST: 20 MINUTES
MAKES 6 ACCOMPANIMENT SERVINGS.

**1 medium head cauliflower
    (2 pounds), cut into 1 1/2" flowerets
1 tablespoon olive oil
1/2 teaspoon salt**

**1/4 teaspoon coarsely ground
    black pepper
2 tablespoons chopped fresh parsley
1 garlic clove, finely chopped**

1. Preheat oven to 450°F. In 15 1/2" by 10 1/2" jelly-roll pan, toss cauliflower with oil, salt, and pepper until evenly coated. Roast cauliflower, stirring halfway through roasting time, until tender, about 20 minutes.

2. In small cup, combine parsley and garlic. Sprinkle over cauliflower and stir to mix evenly. Roast 3 minutes longer. Spoon into serving dish.

*Each serving: About 35 calories, 1g protein, 3g carbohydrate, 2g total fat
(0g saturated), 0mg cholesterol, 202mg sodium.*

Oven-Browned Carrots & Parsnips

A duet of sweet root vegetables is subtly accented by the flavor of fresh lemon peel and orange liqueur. Use two pans—overcrowding will keep vegetables from roasting properly.

PREP: 20 MINUTES   ROAST: 1 HOUR
MAKES 10 ACCOMPANIMENT SERVINGS.

2 pounds carrots, peeled and cut into
   3" by 1/2" sticks
2 pounds parsnips, peeled and cut
   into 3" by 1/2" sticks
4 strips fresh lemon peel
   (3" by 1" each)
2 tablespoons orange-flavor liqueur

1 teaspoon sugar
1/2 teaspoon salt
1/4 teaspoon coarsely ground
   black pepper
3 tablespoons butter or margarine,
   cut into pieces

1. Preheat oven to 425°F. In large bowl, toss carrots and parsnips with lemon peel, liqueur, sugar, salt, and pepper.

2. Divide the mixture between two 15 1/2" by 10 1/2" jelly-roll pans (or use 1 jelly-roll pan and 1 shallow large roasting pan) and dot with butter. Roast vegetables, until tender and browned, about 1 hour, stirring occasionally and rotating pans between upper and lower racks halfway through roasting time.

Each serving: About 135 calories, 2g protein, 24g carbohydrate, 4g total fat (3g saturated), 9mg cholesterol, 190mg sodium.

Oven-Browned Carrots & Parsnips

Roasted Eggplant Dip with Herbs

The fresh flavors of lemon and mint are a perfect match for the baked eggplant in this Mediterranean-style dip.

PREP: 15 MINUTES PLUS COOLING AND DRAINING   ROAST: 1 HOUR
MAKES ABOUT 2 CUPS.

2 small eggplants (1 pound each)
2 garlic cloves, thinly sliced
2 tablespoons olive oil
4 teaspoons fresh lemon juice
1 teaspoon salt

1/4 teaspoon ground black pepper
2 tablespoons chopped fresh parsley
2 tablespoons chopped fresh mint
toasted pita bread wedges

1. Preheat oven to 400°F. With knife, cut slits all over eggplants; insert garlic slices in slits. Place eggplants in 15 1/2" by 10 1/2" jelly-roll pan and roast until collapsed and tender, about 1 hour.

2. When cool enough to handle, cut eggplants in half. Scoop out flesh and place in colander set over bowl; discard skin. Let drain 10 minutes.

3. Transfer eggplant to food processor with knife blade attached. Add oil, lemon juice, salt, and pepper; pulse to coarsely chop. Add parsley and mint, pulse to combine. Spoon mixture into bowl; cover and refrigerate up to 4 hours. Serve with pita bread wedges.

Each tablespoon: About 14 calories, 0g protein, 2g carbohydrate, 1g total fat (0g saturated), 0mg cholesterol, 74mg sodium.

Roasted Fennel

This side dish can't be beat as the perfect partner for fish or pork. Try it with trout or salmon for pure eating pleasure.

PREP: 10 MINUTES   ROAST: 1 HOUR   MAKES 6 ACCOMPANIMENT SERVINGS.

3 medium fennel bulbs (1¼ pounds each), each trimmed and cut into 6 wedges

1 tablespoon olive oil
½ teaspoon salt
¼ teaspoon ground black pepper

1. Preheat oven to 425°F. In 15½" by 10½" jelly-roll pan, toss fennel with oil, salt, and pepper until fennel is evenly coated.

2. Roast fennel until tender and browned at edges, about 1 hour.

Each serving: About 58 calories, 3g protein, 7g carbohydrate, 3g total fat (0g saturated), 0mg cholesterol, 420mg sodium.

Roasted Eggplant Parmesan

Eggplant Parmesan usually requires lots of frying—but not our streamlined recipe.

PREP: 35 MINUTES   ROAST/COOK: 45 MINUTES
MAKES 6 MAIN-DISH SERVINGS.

2 small eggplants (1¼ pounds each), cut into ½-inch-thick slices

¼ cup olive oil

½ teaspoon salt

1 can (28 ounces) plum tomatoes, drained and chopped

¼ teaspoon ground black pepper

⅓ cup chopped fresh parsley

4 ounces mozzarella cheese, shredded (1 cup)

½ cup freshly grated Parmesan cheese

1. Preheat oven to 450°F. Place eggplant on two large cookie sheets. Brush oil on both sides of eggplant and sprinkle with ¼ teaspoon salt. Roast for 15 minutes; turn slices and roast until eggplant has browned and is tender, 20 to 25 minutes.

2. Meanwhile, in nonstick 12-inch skillet, combine tomatoes, remaining ¼ teaspoon salt, and pepper; cook over low heat, stirring occasionally, until tomatoes have thickened, about 20 minutes. Stir in parsley.

3. Turn oven control to 400°F. In shallow 2½-quart casserole, layer half of eggplant and top with half of tomato sauce; sprinkle with half of mozzarella. Repeat layers; top with grated Parmesan. Cover loosely with foil and roast until bubbling, about 10 minutes.

4. Remove casserole from oven and let stand at least 10 minutes before serving. Serve hot or at room temperature.

Each serving: About 248 calories, 11g protein, 19g carbohydrate, 16g total fat (5g saturated), 21mg cholesterol, 693mg sodium.

Caponata

Caponata (which gets its name from the capers in the dish) has an intriguing sweet-and-sour flavor. Serve it as part of a cold antipasto, spread it on bruschetta, or offer it as a first course.

PREP: 30 MINUTES PLUS COOLING   ROAST/COOK: 45 MINUTES
MAKES ABOUT 5 CUPS.

2 small eggplants (1 pound each), ends trimmed and cut into 3/4-inch pieces
1/2 cup extravirgin olive oil
1/4 teaspoon salt
3 small red onions, thinly sliced
1 1/2 pounds ripe tomatoes (4 medium), peeled, seeded, and chopped
1 cup olives, such as Gaeta, green Sicilian, or Kalamata, pitted and chopped

3 tablespoons capers, drained
3 tablespoons golden raisins
1/4 teaspoon coarsely ground black pepper
4 stalks celery with leaves, thinly sliced
1/3 cup red wine vinegar
2 teaspoons sugar
1/4 cup chopped fresh parsley

1. Preheat oven to 450°F. Divide eggplant between two 15 1/2" by 10 1/2" jelly-roll pans. Drizzle with 1/4 cup oil and sprinkle with salt; toss to coat. Roast the eggplant 10 minutes. Stir, then roast until browned, about 10 minutes longer.

2. Meanwhile, in nonstick 12-inch skillet, heat remaining 1/4 cup oil over medium heat. Add onions and cook, stirring, until tender and golden, about 10 minutes. Add tomatoes, olives, capers, raisins, and pepper. Reduce heat; cover and simmer 15 minutes.

3. Add eggplant and celery to skillet and cook over medium heat, stirring, until celery is just tender, 8 to 10 minutes. Stir in vinegar and sugar and cook 1 minute longer. Cool to room temperature, or cover and refrigerate up to overnight. To serve, sprinkle with parsley.

Each 1/4 cup: About 106 calories, 1g protein, 9g carbohydrate, 8g total fat (1g saturated), 0mg cholesterol, 336mg sodium.

Roasted Garlic

When garlic is roasted, it turns into a soft, spreadable paste with a tantalizingly sweet, mellow flavor. Try it the classic way—spread on grilled or toasted country-style bread. Or, do as chefs do: Toss some of the garlic with cooked vegetables or hot pasta; stir into soups, mashed potatoes, or rice; or spread on grilled meat, poultry, or seafood.

PREP: 10 MINUTES PLUS COOLING   ROAST: 1 HOUR
MAKES ABOUT 1 1/4 CUPS.

4 heads garlic
2 tablespoons extravirgin olive oil
1/8 teaspoon salt

1/8 teaspoon coarsely ground black pepper
4 fresh thyme sprigs

1. Preheat oven to 350°F. Remove any loose papery skin from the garlic, leaving heads intact. Place garlic on sheet of heavy-duty foil; drizzle with oil and sprinkle with salt and pepper. Place 1 thyme sprig on top of each head.
2. Loosely wrap foil around garlic, folding foil edges securely to keep in oil. Roast until garlic has softened, about 1 hour. Transfer packet to plate. Open carefully and discard foil and herb sprigs.
3. When cool enough to handle, separate garlic into cloves. Squeeze soft garlic from each clove into small bowl.

Each tablespoon: About 25 calories, 1g protein, 3g carbohydrate, 1g total fat (0g saturated), 0mg cholesterol, 16mg sodium.

Sweet Roasted Onions

A great accompaniment to turkey and all the other fixings, these onions are roasted with brown sugar and a splash of vinegar. If not serving right away, arrange cooked onion slices in shallow 2-quart microwave- or oven-safe baking dish; cover and refrigerate up to 2 days. Reheat, covered, in microwave oven until hot or in 350°F oven 30 minutes.

PREP: 20 MINUTES   ROAST: 1 HOUR 35 MINUTES
MAKES 12 ACCOMPANIMENT SERVINGS.

2 jumbo red onions (about 1 pound each), each cut into ³/₄-inch-thick rounds	3 tablespoons olive oil
	¹/₂ teaspoon salt
	2 tablespoons brown sugar
2 jumbo white or yellow onions (about 1 pound each), each cut into ³/₄-inch-thick rounds	1 tablespoon cider vinegar
	fresh thyme leaves

1. Preheat oven to 400°F. Keeping slices intact, arrange red-onion slices in single layer in 15¹/₂" by 10¹/₂" jelly-roll pan; arrange white-onion slices in single layer in separate jelly-roll pan or large cookie sheet.

2. With pastry brush, coat both sides of onions with oil, and sprinkle with salt. Roast onions 45 minutes.

3. With spatula, turn over onion slices. Rotate pans between upper and lower racks of oven; roast onions until tender and golden, about 30 minutes longer.

4. Meanwhile, in cup, mix sugar and vinegar. Brush onions with sugar mixture, and roast 5 minutes longer.

5. With wide metal spatula, turn onion slices (the undersides look more golden), and arrange, alternating red and white onion slices, overlapping slightly, in serving dish. Sprinkle with thyme leaves.

Each serving: About 90 calories, 2g protein, 14g carbohydrate, 4g total fat (1g saturated), 0mg cholesterol, 100mg sodium.

How to Roast a Pepper

Nothing quite compares to a plump roasted pepper drizzled with olive oil and sprinkled with salt and pepper. Our easy roasting method doesn't involve long oven time and a lot of patience but still makes tender, delicious charred peppers for salad plates and pasta tosses. Red peppers are also a good source of vitamin C.

1. Preheat broiler. Line broiling pan (without rack) with foil. Cut each pepper lengthwise in half; remove and discard stems and seeds. Trim thick white membrane. Arrange pepper halves, cut side down, in prepared broiling pan. With hand, flatten each.

2. Place pan in broiler. Broil, without turning, 5 to 6 inches from heat source until skin is charred and blistered, about 10 to 15 minutes.

3. Wrap peppers in foil from broiling pan and allow them to steam at room temperature 15 minutes or until cool enough to handle. Remove peppers from foil. Peel skin and discard.

To roast peppers outdoors:

Prepare grill. Follow Step 1, then place pepper halves, cut side up, on grill rack. Cook until charred, then wrap in foil and follow Step 3.

Roasted Red Pepper Puree

Spread this luscious puree on slices of toasted French bread for a tasty hors d'oeuvre, or dollop it into soup like minestrone or bouillabaise.

PREP: 10 MINUTES PLUS COOLING   ROAST: 10 TO 15 MINUTES
MAKES ABOUT 2/3 CUP.

2 medium red peppers	1 teaspoon fennel seeds, crushed
1 slice whole-wheat or white bread,	1/2 teaspoon salt
torn into bite-size pieces	1/8 teaspoon coarsely ground black
1 tablespoon olive oil	pepper
1/2 small garlic clove	1 tablespoon water

1. Preheat broiler. Line broiling pan (without rack) with foil. Cut each pepper lengthwise in half; discard stems and seeds. Place peppers, cut side down, in broiling pan. With hand, flatten each. Place pan in broiler 5 to 6 inches from heat source. Broil peppers, without turning, until skin is charred and blistered, 10 to 15 minutes. Wrap peppers in foil from broiling pan and allow to steam at room temperature or until cool enough to handle, about 15 minutes. Remove the peppers from the foil; peel skin and discard.

2. Cut roasted peppers into bite-size pieces; place in mini food processor with sharp side of blade facing up, or in blender. Add bread, oil, garlic, fennel seeds, salt, pepper, and water and puree, scraping bowl occasionally with rubber spatula, until smooth. Cover and refrigerate up to three days if not serving right away.

Each tablespoon: About 25 calories, 1g protein, 3g carbohydrate, 1g total fat (0g saturated), 0mg cholesterol, 120mg sodium.

Roasted Baby Potatoes with Herbs

Oven–roasting concentrates the wonderful flavor in these small baby potatoes.

PREP: 10 MINUTES   ROAST: 30 MINUTES

MAKES: 6 ACCOMPANIMENT SERVINGS.

1 1/2 pounds very small red, white, or yellow potatoes (if using larger potatoes, cut each into quarters or eighths)
1 tablespoon olive oil
1/2 teaspoon salt
2 green onions, trimmed and thinly sliced
2 tablespoons minced fresh dill
1 tablespoon minced fresh mint

1. Preheat oven to 450°F. In medium roasting pan (14" by 10"), toss the potatoes with oil and salt. Roast potatoes, stirring once halfway through roasting time, until fork–tender and golden, about 25 minutes.

2. Sprinkle potatoes with green onions, dill, and mint; toss to combine. Roast potatoes 5 minutes longer.

Each serving: About 120 calories, 2g protein, 23g carbohydrate, 2g total fat (0g saturated), 0mg cholesterol, 200mg sodium.

Baby Potatoes with Rosemary

For the best golden-brown potatoes, roast them with olive oil and herbs in a hot oven. Instead of baby potatoes, you can also use larger potatoes cut into bite-size pieces.

PREP: 20 MINUTES   ROAST: 30 TO 40 MINUTES
MAKES 10 ACCOMPANIMENT SERVINGS.

5 pounds assorted small potatoes,
such as red, white, purple, or
golden, cut in half
1/4 cup olive oil
2 tablespoons chopped fresh
rosemary or thyme or 1 teaspoon
dried rosemary or thyme

1 1/2 teaspoons salt
1/2 teaspoon coarsely ground
black pepper

Preheat oven to 425°F. In large roasting pan (17" by 11 1/2"), toss potatoes with oil, rosemary, salt, and pepper until potatoes are evenly coated. Roast potatoes, turning occasionally, until golden and tender, 30 to 40 minutes.

Each serving: About 232 calories, 4g protein, 41g carbohydrate, 6g total fat (1g saturated), 0mg cholesterol, 366mg sodium.

Oven Fries

You won't miss the fat in these hand-cut "fries." They bake beautifully on a jelly-roll pan with a spritz of nonstick cooking spray and a sprinkle of salt and pepper.

PREP: 10 MINUTES   BAKE: 20 TO 25 MINUTES
MAKES 4 ACCOMPANIMENT SERVINGS.

Nonstick cooking spray
3 medium baking potatoes
  (8 ounces each)

1/2 teaspoon salt
1/4 teaspoon coarsely ground
  black pepper

1. Preheat the oven to 500°F. Spray two 15 1/2" by 10 1/2" jelly-roll pans or 2 large cookie sheets with nonstick cooking spray.

2. Scrub unpeeled potatoes well, but do not peel. Cut each potato lengthwise in half. With each potato half cut side down, cut lengthwise into 1/4-inch-thick slices. Place potatoes in medium bowl and toss with salt and pepper.

3. Divide potato slices between pans and spray potatoes with nonstick cooking spray. Roast potatoes until tender and lightly browned, about 20 minutes, rotating pans between upper and lower racks halfway through roasting time.

Each serving: About 130 calories, 4g protein, 28g carbohydrate, 1g total fat (0g saturated), 0mg cholesterol, 280mg sodium.

Rosemary & Garlic Oven Fries

Prepare Oven Fries as above, but in Step 3 add 1/2 **teaspoon dried rosemary,** crumbled, and **2 garlic cloves,** crushed with garlic press.

Rosemary & Garlic Oven Fries

Pan-Roasted Potatoes

While roasting meat or poultry in the oven, pop in these potatoes. They'll turn out crispy on the outside and tender on the inside. If your oven temperature is lower than 350°F, just cook the potatoes a little bit longer.

PREP: 10 MINUTES   ROAST: 1 HOUR 30 MINUTES
MAKES 6 ACCOMPANIMENT SERVINGS.

6 medium all-purpose or baking potatoes (6 ounces each), each peeled and cut in half

2 tablespoons olive oil
$1/2$ teaspoon salt

Preheat oven to 350°F. In small roasting pan (13" by 9"), toss potatoes with oil until evenly coated. Arrange potatoes, cut side down, in pan. Roast until tender and golden, about 1 hour 30 minutes. Sprinkle with salt.

Each serving: About 129 calories, 2g protein, 20g carbohydrate, 5g total fat (1g saturated), 0mg cholesterol, 200mg sodium.

Balsamic-Roasted Sweet Potato Wedges

We brushed these sweet potatoes with a balsamic vinegar–based glaze for extra kick.

PREP: 15 MINUTES   ROAST: 45 MINUTES
MAKES 12 ACCOMPANIMENT SERVINGS.

5 pounds (8 medium) sweet potatoes, peeled and each cut lengthwise into 8 wedges
2/3 cup packed light brown sugar

1/3 cup balsamic vinegar
3 tablespoons butter or margarine
3/4 teaspoon salt
1/4 cup water

1. Preheat oven to 400°F. Divide sweet potatoes between two 15 1/2" by 10 1/2" jelly-roll pans. In 1-quart saucepan, heat brown sugar, vinegar, butter, salt, and water to boiling over high heat. Drizzle sugar mixture over potatoes; toss to coat. Spread potatoes evenly in pans.

2. Roast potatoes, turning potatoes occasionally to coat, until very tender and glaze has thickened, about 45 minutes.

Each serving: About 230 calories, 3g protein, 50g carbohydrate, 3g total fat (2g saturated), 8mg cholesterol, 196mg sodium.

Glazed Parsnips

Roasted parsnips can be served with almost any meat or poultry. They are at their peak of flavor in the autumn, just in time for the holidays.

PREP: 15 MINUTES   ROAST: 45 MINUTES
MAKES 12 ACCOMPANIMENT SERVINGS.

5 pounds parsnips, peeled   **$1/2$ teaspoon salt**
2 tablespoons sugar   **$1/8$ teaspoon ground black pepper**
2 tablespoons olive oil

1. Preheat oven to 425°F. Cut parsnips crosswise into 3" pieces. Cut pieces lengthwise in half or into quarters if thick. In nonstick 15$1/2$" by 10$1/2$" jelly-roll pan, toss parsnips with sugar, oil, salt, and pepper until evenly coated. Transfer half of parsnips to another nonstick jelly-roll pan or shallow large roasting pan.

2. Roast parsnips, tossing occasionally, until tender and glazed, for about 45 minutes, rotating the pans between upper and lower racks halfway through roasting.

Each serving: About 150 calories, 2g protein, 31g carbohydrate, 3g total fat (0g saturated), 0mg cholesterol, 115mg sodium.

Roasted Buttercup Squash

High in beta-carotene and flavor, this buttercup squash is a great accompaniment for cold-weather meals.

Prep: 10 minutes   Roast: 1 hour
Makes 4 accompaniment servings.

1 large buttercup squash (3 pounds),
  cut into quarters and seeded
4 teaspoons butter or margarine

¹/₈ teaspoon salt
pinch ground black pepper

1. Preheat oven to 400°F. Place squash, cut side down, in 15¹/₂" by 10¹/₂" jelly-roll pan; pour ¹/₄ *inch water* into pan. Roast 45 minutes.
2. Turn squash cut side up. Place one-fourth of butter, salt, and pepper into each cavity. Roast until very tender, about 15 minutes longer.

Each serving: About 163 calories, 3g protein, 33g carbohydrate, 4g total fat (2g saturated), 10mg cholesterol, 124mg sodium.

Rosemary-Roasted Butternut Squash

Hearty chunks of winter squash become aromatic and sweet when roasted with rosemary.

PREP: 10 MINUTES ROAST: 35 MINUTES
MAKES 6 ACCOMPANIMENT SERVINGS.

3 tablespoons butter or margarine
1 large butternut squash (3 pounds)
1 medium onion, chopped
1¼ teaspoons salt

¾ teaspoon dried rosemary, crumbled
¼ teaspoon coarsely ground black pepper

1. Preheat oven to 400°F. Place butter in small roasting pan (13" by 9"); place pan in oven until butter melts. Meanwhile, cut squash lengthwise in half; discard seeds. With vegetable peeler, remove peel, then cut squash into 2-inch pieces.

2. In large bowl, combine onion, salt, rosemary, and pepper. Add squash and toss to coat. Add squash mixture to melted butter in pan; toss to coat. Arrange squash in single layer and roast until tender, about 35 minutes.

Each serving: About 148 calories, 2g protein, 25g carbohydrate, 6g total fat (4g saturated), 16mg cholesterol, 551mg sodium.

Roasted Sunchokes

Roasting brings out the subtle nutty flavor of this knobby tuber. Serve with roast beef or as part of an assortment of roasted vegetables.

PREP: 15 MINUTES ROAST: 1 HOUR
MAKES 8 ACCOMPANIMENT SERVINGS.

2 pounds sunchokes (Jerusalem artichokes)
1 tablespoon olive oil
1 teaspoon salt
1/4 teaspoon ground black pepper
chopped fresh parsley

1. Preheat oven to 425°F. With vegetable brush, scrub sunchokes under cold running water. In medium roasting pan (14" by 10"), toss sunchokes with oil, salt, and pepper until evenly coated.

2. Roast sunchokes until tender, about 1 hour. To serve, sprinkle with the chopped parsley.

Each serving: About 75 calories, 2g protein, 14g carbohydrate, 2g total fat (0g saturated), 0mg cholesterol, 294mg sodium.

Garlic-Crumbed Tomatoes

Garlic-Crumbed Tomatoes

What could be simpler or yummier than this favorite summer side dish?

PREP: 20 MINUTES   ROAST: 15 MINUTES
MAKES 4 ACCOMPANIMENT SERVINGS.

2 tablespoons butter or margarine
1 garlic clove, crushed with
   garlic press
1/2 cup fresh bread crumbs
1/4 cup loosely packed fresh parsley
   or basil leaves, chopped

1/4 cup grated Parmesan cheese
1/4 teaspoon salt
1/8 teaspoon ground black pepper
2 ripe large tomatoes (12 ounces
   each), cored and cut crosswise
   in half

1. Arrange oven rack in upper third of oven. Preheat oven to 425°F. Line broiling pan (without rack) or cookie sheet with foil.
2. In 10-inch skillet, melt butter over medium heat. Add garlic and cook, stirring, until fragrant, about 1 minute. Remove skillet from heat; stir in bread crumbs, parsley, Parmesan, salt, and pepper.
3. Place tomato halves, cut side up, in prepared pan. Top tomatoes with crumb mixture. Roast until tomatoes are heated through and topping is golden, about 15 minutes.

Each serving: About 125 calories, 4g protein, 11g carbohydrate, 8g total fat (4g saturated), 20mg cholesterol, 342mg sodium.

Oven-Roasted Tomatoes

Typical oven-dried tomatoes can take hours. Not ours. Add to sandwiches or use for a tomato bruschetta topped with goat cheese and fresh basil.

PREP: 15 MINUTES   ROAST: 25 MINUTES
MAKES ABOUT 24 DRIED TOMATO HALVES.

3 pounds plum tomatoes (about 12 large)
2 teaspoons plus 2 tablespoons olive oil
1/2 teaspoon salt

1/4 teaspoon coarsely ground black pepper
1 garlic clove, crushed with garlic press

1. Preheat oven to 450°F. Line two 15 1/2" by 10 1/2" jelly-roll pans or large cookie sheets with foil. Cut each tomato lengthwise in half; with small spoon, scoop out seeds and discard. Pat insides dry with paper towels.

2. In large bowl, with spatula, toss tomatoes with 2 teaspoons oil.

3. Arrange tomatoes, cut side down, on prepared pans. Roast until shriveled and browned, 25 to 30 minutes, rotating pans between upper and lower racks halfway through roasting time. Cool tomatoes slightly in pans on wire racks.

4. When tomatoes are cool enough to handle, remove and discard skins. Gently toss tomatoes with salt, pepper, garlic, and remaining 2 tablespoons oil. Cool tomatoes completely. Store tomatoes in ziptight plastic bag in the refrigerator up to 3 days, or in the freezer up to 6 months.

Each tomato half: About 25 calories, 1g protein, 3g carbohydrate, 2g total fat (0g saturated), 0mg cholesterol, 55mg sodium.

Roasted Cherry Tomatoes with Lime

A delicious accompaniment to roast beef, lamb, or chicken. If your gang likes spice, be sure to add the cardamom.

Prep: 5 minutes   Roast: 15 minutes
Makes 4 accompaniment servings.

2 pints red and/or yellow pear, grape, or small cherry tomatoes
1 tablespoon olive oil
1/2 teaspoon ground cardamom (optional)

1/4 teaspoon salt
1/4 teaspoon coarsely ground pepper
1 lime

1. Preheat oven to 450°F.
2. In 15 1/2" by 10 1/2" jelly-roll pan, toss tomatoes with olive oil, cardamom (if using), salt, and pepper. Roast tomatoes, shaking the pan twice, until skins split, about 15 minutes.
3. Meanwhile, from the lime, grate 1/4 teaspoon peel and squeeze 1 tablespoon juice.
4. Transfer tomatoes with their juice to serving bowl; stir in lime peel and juice. Serve tomatoes hot or at room temperature.

Each serving: About 65 calories, 2g protein, 8g carbohydrate, 4g total fat (1g saturated), 0mg cholesterol, 160mg sodium.

Roasted Chestnuts

Chestnuts are an integral part of cold-weather cooking and can be presented in many guises: in almost any stuffing, added to your favorite vegetable medley, or pureed with sugar and vanilla and served with softly whipped cream for a special dessert.

PREP: 30 MINUTES   ROAST: 20 MINUTES   MAKES 2 CUPS.

1 pound fresh chestnuts

1. Preheat oven to 400°F. With sharp knife, cut an X in flat side of shell of each chestnut. Place in 15 1/2" by 10 1/2" jelly-roll pan and roast chestnuts until shells open, about 20 minutes.

2. Cover chestnuts with clean kitchen towel. When cool enough to handle, with paring knife, peel hot chestnuts, keeping unpeeled chestnuts warm for easier peeling.

Each 1/2 cup: About 179 calories, 2g protein, 38g carbohydrate, 2g total fat (0g saturated), 0mg cholesterol, 3mg sodium.

With a sharp knife, cut an X in the flat side of each chestnut.

With paring knife peel hot chestnuts.

Double-Roasted Spiced Nuts

Prep: 10 minutes plus cooling   Roast: 35 minutes
Makes about 4 1/3 cups.

1 cup blanched whole almonds
1 cup pecan halves
1 cup hazelnuts (filberts)
1 large egg white
1/3 cup sugar

2 teaspoons ground cinnamon
1 teaspoon ground allspice
1/2 teaspoon ground nutmeg
1/2 teaspoon salt

1. Preheat oven to 350°F. In 15 1/2" by 10 1/2" jelly-roll pan, spread almonds and pecans. In 8" by 8" metal baking pan, spread hazelnuts. Roast nuts 12 to 15 minutes or until toasted, stirring once. Cool almonds and pecans in pan on wire rack. Remove skins from hazelnuts by wrapping hot nuts in clean cloth towel; with hands, roll hazelnuts back and forth in towel until as much of the skin as possible rubs off. Do not turn oven off.

2. In medium bowl, with wire whisk, beat egg white until foamy. Add sugar, cinnamon, allspice, nutmeg, salt, and *2 teaspoons water*, and beat until well combined. Add nuts to egg-white mixture; stir until the nuts are well coated.

3. Spray same jelly-roll pan with *nonstick cooking spray*. Spread nut mixture evenly in pan. Roast 20 minutes or until coating on nuts becomes firm and opaque, stirring once. Cool completely in pan on wire rack. Break any clusters of nuts apart. Store nuts in tightly covered container up to 2 weeks.

Each 1/4 cup: About 150 calories, 3g protein, 8g carbohydrate, 13g total fat (1g saturated), 2g fiber, 0mg cholesterol, 70mg sodium.

Roasted Vanilla Pears

The fragrant vanilla syrup has a hint of lemon and caramelizes slightly during roasting. If not using vanilla bean, increase the lemon peel to 3 strips and stir 2 teaspoons vanilla extract into syrup after the pears have been roasted.

PREP: 25 MINUTES PLUS COOLING   ROAST: 35 TO 40 MINUTES
MAKES 8 SERVINGS.

1 lemon	1/2 cup sugar
1 whole vanilla bean	2 tablespoons butter, melted (do
8 firm but ripe Bosc pears (about	not use margarine)
3 1/2 pounds), unpeeled	1/2 cup water

1. Preheat oven to 450°F. From lemon, with vegetable peeler or small knife, remove two 2" by 1" strips of peel. Squeeze 1 tablespoon juice from lemon. Cut vanilla bean crosswise in half, then cut each half lengthwise, without cutting all the way through to the other side. With knife, scrape out seeds. Reserve seeds and pod.

2. With melon baller or small knife, remove core and blossom end (bottom) of each pear, but do not remove stems. If necessary, cut thin slice from bottom of each pear so it will stand upright. Sprinkle 1/2 teaspoon sugar into cored area of each pear; swirl pears to coat insides with sugar. With pastry brush, brush pears with some melted butter; set aside.

3. In shallow 10-inch round ceramic or glass baking dish, mix lemon-peel strips, lemon juice, vanilla-bean pod, vanilla seeds, remaining sugar, any remaining melted butter, and water. Stand the pears, cored end down, in baking dish.

4. Roast pears, basting occasionally with syrup in dish, until fork-tender, 35 to 40 minutes.

5. Cool pears slightly to serve warm. Or cool completely and cover and refrigerate up to 1 day. Reheat to serve warm, if you like.

Each serving: About 160 calories, 1g protein, 34g carbohydrate, 3g total fat (2g saturated), 8mg cholesterol, 30mg sodium.

Roasted Apples with Ice Cream

Put them in the oven just before you begin to eat and dessert will be ready when you are.

PREP: 15 MINUTES   ROAST: 20 MINUTES   MAKES 6 SERVINGS.

4 tablespoons butter or margarine
3/4 cup packed light brown sugar
1/3 cup golden raisins
2 tablespoons fresh lemon juice
2 tablespoons Calvados (apple brandy), apple juice, or water

1 1/2 pounds Granny Smith apples (6 small), each cut in half and cored
1 1/2 pints vanilla ice cream

1. Preheat oven to 425°F.

2. In 2-quart saucepan, melt butter over medium heat. Add sugar, raisins, lemon juice, and Calvados, and cook, stirring constantly, until the sugar has melted.

3. Pour sugar mixture into 15 1/2" by 10 1/2" jelly-roll pan; arrange apples, cut sides down, in pan. Roast, without turning, until apples are very soft, about 20 minutes.

4. Serve warm apples and their syrup with ice cream.

Each serving: About 425 calories, 3g protein, 66g carbohydrate, 18g total fat (7g saturated), 35mg cholesterol, 145mg sodium.

Roasted Apples with Ice Cream

INDEX

PHOTOGRAPHY CREDITS

Page 2: Alan Richardson
Page 3: Ann Stratton
Page 6: Ann Stratton
Page 8: Rita Maas
Page 12: Brian Hagiwara
Page 15: Alan Richardson
Page 21: Steven Mark Needham
Page 25: Steven Mark Needham
Page 33: Brian Hagiwara
Page 41: Alan Richardson
Page 44: Rita Maas
Page 49: Alan Richardson
Page 50: Brian Hagiwara
Page 55: Brian Hagiwara
Page 62: Ann Stratton
Page 65: Brian Hagiwara
Page 68: Brian Hagiwara
Page 73: Ann Stratton
Page 78: William Meppem
Page 83: Ann Stratton
Page 87: Alan Richardson
Page 90: Brian Hagiwara
Page 104: Brian Hagiwara

Page 107: Mark Thomas
Page 108: Mark Thomas
Page 111: Rita Maas
Page 117: Brian Hagiwara
Page 129: Mark Thomas
Page 138: Mark Thomas
Page 141: Alan Richardson
Page 147: Mark Thomas
Page 151: Brian Hagiwara
Page 155: Mark Thomas
Page 160: Alan Richardson
Page 164: Brian Hagiwara
Page 167: Mark Thomas
Page 171: Brian Hagiwara
Page 174: Mark Thomas
Page 178: Mark Thomas
Page 187: Mark Thomas
Page 199: Ann Stratton
Page 206: Brian Hagiwara
Page 211: Rita Maas
Page 215: Sang An
Page 224: William Meppem

METRIC CONVERSION CHART

The recipes that appear in this cookbook use the standard United States method for measuring liquid and dry or solid ingredients (teaspoons, tablespoons, and cups). The information on this chart is provided to help cooks outside the U.S. successfully use these recipes. All equivalents are approximate.

METRIC EQUIVALENTS FOR DIFFERENT TYPES OF INGREDIENTS

A standard cup measure of a dry or solid ingredient will vary in weight depending on the type of ingredient. A standard cup of liquid is the same volume for any type of liquid. Use the following chart when converting standard cup measures to grams (weight) or milliliters (volume).

Standard Cup	Fine Powder (e.g. flour)	Grain (e.g. rice)	Granular (e.g. sugar)	Liquid Solids (e.g. butter)	Liquid (e.g. milk)
1	140 g	150 g	190 g	200 g	240 ml
$3/4$	105 g	113 g	143 g	150 g	180 ml
$2/3$	93 g	100 g	125 g	133 g	160 ml
$1/2$	70 g	75 g	95 g	100 g	120 ml
$1/3$	47 g	50 g	63 g	67 g	80 ml
$1/4$	35 g	38 g	48 g	50 g	60 ml
$1/8$	18 g	19 g	24 g	25 g	30 ml

USEFUL EQUIVALENTS FOR LIQUID INGREDIENTS BY VOLUME

$1/4$ tsp =				1 ml
$1/2$ tsp =				2 ml
1 tsp =				5 ml
3 tsp =	1 tbls =		$1/2$ fl oz =	15 ml
	2 tbls =	$1/8$ cup =	1 fl oz =	30 ml
	4 tbls =	$1/4$ cup =	2 fl oz =	60 ml
	5 $1/3$ tbls =	$1/3$ cup =	3 fl oz =	80 ml
	8 tbls =	$1/2$ cup =	4 fl oz =	120 ml
	10 $2/3$ tbls =	$2/3$ cup =	5 fl oz =	160 ml
	12 tbls =	$3/4$ cup =	6 fl oz =	180 ml
	16 tbls =	1 cup =	8 fl oz =	240 ml
	1 pt =	2 cups =	16 fl oz =	480 ml
	1 qt =	4 cups =	32 fl oz =	960 ml
			33 fl oz =	1000 ml = 1l

USEFUL EQUIVALENTS FOR DRY INGREDIENTS BY WEIGHT
(To convert ounces to grams, multiply the number of ounces by 30.)

1 oz =	$1/16$ lb =	30 g
4 oz =	$1/4$ lb =	120 g
8 oz =	$1/2$ lb =	240 g
12 oz =	$3/4$ lb =	360 g
16 oz =	1 lb =	480 g

USEFUL EQUIVALENTS FOR LENGTH
(To convert inches to centimeters, multiply the number of inches by 2.5.)

1 in =			2.5 cm
6 in =	$1/2$ ft =		15 cm
12 in =	1 ft =		30 cm
36 in =	3 ft =	1 yd =	90 cm
40 in =			100 cm = 1 m

USEFUL EQUIVALENTS FOR COOKING/OVEN TEMPERATURES

	Fahrenheit	Celsius	Gas Mark
Freeze Water	32° F	0° C	
Room Temperature	68° F	20° C	
Boil Water	212° F	100° C	
Bake	325° F	160° C	3
	350° F	180° C	4
	375° F	190° C	5
	400° F	200° C	6
	425° F	220° C	7
	450° F	230° C	8
Broil			Grill